Transforming Special Education Practices

A Primer for School Administrators and Policy Makers

Edited by
Peter J. Bittel and Nicholas D. Young

Published in partnership with the
American Association of School Administrators

ROWMAN & LITTLEFIELD EDUCATION
A division of
ROWMAN & LITTLEFIELD PUBLISHERS, INC.
Lanham • New York • Toronto • Plymouth, UK

Published in partnership with the American Association of School Administrators

Published by Rowman & Littlefield Education
A division of Rowman & Littlefield Publishers, Inc.
A wholly owned subsidary of The Rowman & Littlefield Publishing Group, Inc.
4501 Forbes Boulevard, Suite 200, Lanham, Maryland 20706
www.rowman.com

10 Thornbury Road, Plymouth PL6 7PP, United Kingdom

British Library Cataloguing in Publication Information Available

Library of Congress Cataloging-in-Publication Data

Transforming special education practices : a primer for school administrators and policy makers / edited by Nicholas D. Young and Peter J. Bittel.
p. cm.
Includes bibliographical references.
ISBN 978-1-61048-854-9 (cloth : alk. paper) -- ISBN 978-1-61048-855-6 (pbk. : alk. paper) -- ISBN 978-1-61048-856-3 (electronic)
1. Special education--United States--Administration. 2. Special education--Law and legislation--United States. 3. School management and organization--United States. I. Young, Nicholas D., 1967- II. Bittel, Peter J., 1948-
LC3981.U75 2012
371.9--dc23
2012025091

The paper used in this publication meets the minimum requirements of American National Standard for Information Sciences Permanence of Paper for Printed Library Materials, ANSI/NISO Z39.48-1992.

Printed in the United States of America

Contents

Acknowledgments

We are indebted to our "community of practitioners" who helped us assemble this book. We appreciate their efforts, intelligence, insights, and dedication to the field of special education. Because we assembled a group of writers who "get it," we believe the reader will readily glean practical information as a result of our collective expertise. In particular, the keen editorial expertise of Dr. Jane Miller and Dr. Dominick C. Vita has been invaluable.

The staff at Futures Education has provided valuable supports for the foundation of this book. Brian Edwards, Michael Neiman, Kindreth Stoia, and Michelle Lynch have offered their insight and editorial expertise to the endeavor, making the book a better document.

Futures Education, a division of the Futures HealthCore, is a private educational partner conducting services for over 200 public school districts nationwide. It is headquartered in Springfield, Massachusetts, with offices in locations across the country. Futures Education partners with public schools in identifying effectiveness and accountability opportunities in special education delivery systems.

We would like to recognize two of our colleagues for their considerable support in the completion of this book:

Dr. Richard Holzman has provided suggestions, encouragement, and guidance from his more than thirty years as a superintendent.

Dr. Tom Scott, executive director of the Massachusetts Association of School Superintendents (MASS), has been a guiding light for all of us working in special education. Dr. Scott's focus on practicality, responsibility, and common sense is remarkable in the conversation about education in America.

We would like to thank all of you who believe that we need to do better work for our students with disabilities than we have ever done before.

—Peter J. Bittel, EdD, and Nicholas D. Young, PhD, EdD

Introduction

The complex and competing demands facing superintendents of American public education have significantly increased in recent years. Superintendents often report that the array of mandated special education programs, the demands of No Child Left Behind (NCLB), and the re-authorization of the Elementary and Secondary Education Act (ESEA) are primary reasons for the increased demand. Specifically, superintendents' responsibilities are now more complex due to the mandates associated with NCLB, IDEA, and Section 504 of the Rehabilitation Act of 1973.

New educational laws and mandates require the superintendent to navigate politically charged environments, responding to competing stakeholders within an increasingly transparent environment of accountability and regulation. In addition, there is considerable demand from all stakeholders wanting quantifiable outcome data concerning student achievement and system organizational performance.

Federal laws and regulations require each state to assess the effectiveness of special education services offered in their schools and districts through auditing compliance with established performance indicators as well as by tracking student outcome measures. This book was developed by practitioners with expertise in both general and special education, to serve as a resource for superintendents in meeting accountability benchmarks while positively transforming special education practices.

STATE OF SPECIAL EDUCATION PROGRAMMING

The United States initiated an effort never before undertaken in the history of civilized man: a commitment to educate *all students*. This commitment brings considerable urgency to the need to rethink special education leadership in relation to programmatic components and fiscal accountability. Nationally, well over $100 billion is spent on special education programs and services. Special education students represent 13.3% of the total school population,[1] yet many districts spend between 20% and 30% of their budget on special education. The expenditures occur despite the fact that almost half of students receiving special education services spend 80% of their day in general education classes. Per pupil, special education costs are 1.9 times the cost of general education.

Despite the disproportionate resources devoted to educating students with disabilities, the success of the effort is suspect. A study conducted by the National Center on Secondary Education Transition in 2008 noted:

- Only 54% of all students with disabilities graduate with a regular diploma;
- Although the graduation rate for all students is 83%, the rate is 66% for students with learning disabilities;[2]
- 49% of students with emotional disabilities drop out of school without a diploma or certificate;
- 24% of students with intellectual disabilities drop out of school without a diploma or certificate.

A national longitudinal study of special education students conducted by the National Center on Secondary Education Transition found only 32% were employed after completing their high school program. During the first year after high school, more than one in four special education students had never held a paying job, nor had they enrolled even part-time in college or job training programs.

Special education students graduate from high school at a rate lower than their non-disabled peers. As a result of such poor outcomes, state and federal regulatory agencies have increased emphasis on preparation for transition planning and post-secondary education, along with tracking data on graduation rates in both general and special education. In September of 2007, the Civil Rights Project at Harvard University's report *Racial Inequity in Special Education* stated that special education placement can contribute to a denial of equality of opportunity for minority students. Partially due to the over-prescription of special education services and supports, 70% or more of African American young men do not graduate from high school with their peers in many large cities.

Disproportional representation of minorities in special education is an increasingly significant problem. State and federal mandates are designed to assure appropriate identification and early intervention services. Such services address the concern that students identified for special education are not simply victims of a lack of appropriate general education instruction.

In his book *Race to Incarcerate*, author Marc Mauer contends that the social consequences of poverty and race are vividly apparent as a continuum beginning with over-identification of minority students for special education and ultimately affecting prison population statistics. If minority students were maintained in general education at rates comparable to those of non-minority students, dropout rates would decline, graduation rates would rise, and the school-to-prison pipeline would flow less swiftly.

The urgency of managing both the fiscal and programmatic aspects of the special education delivery system is growing in the current era of diminishing resources. However, the available literature on the role of the superintendent in special education leadership does not offer pragmatic frameworks to effect change. As practitioners and authors, we felt that the best support in navigating the intricacies, pitfalls, and logistics of special education for superintendents is peer insight from those that have "lived the life." This book was written *by* practitioners *for* practitioners.

PRACTITIONER FOCUS ON RELEVANT CHALLENGES

We asked our contributing authors to write about topics that represent challenges in the special education arena. These reflections offer superintendents an insightful, researched-based guide in understanding the nuances of special education leadership.

From a global perspective, this book examines the changing role of the superintendent in relation to special education leadership demands. Ultimately, the utility of this book will be judged on the degree to which it assists the superintendents in developing cogent strategies resulting in positive outcomes in special education. Below is a brief description of each chapter.

Chapter 1, "*The Superintendent's Role in Special Education Leadership*," provides a practical overview and leadership guide for superintendents. Superintendents have been referred to as the world's "largest piñatas." They answer to a diverse public with varied and, at times, competing agendas. Many superintendents delegate all management of special education services, justifying such delegation based upon the specificity of state and federal mandates and regulatory oversight. As a result, decisions are often made at the building level. The authors consider this distancing to be a fatal flaw. Chapter 1 provides a framework to address the changing role of the superintendent.

Chapter 2, "*Organizational, Personnel, and Fiscal Considerations in the Oversight of Special Education Services*," provides the reader an overview of managing personnel in the special education department. Critical and costly decisions are made daily. Former superintendent Dominick C. Vita and Futures Education's chief operating officer Brian Edwards provide insights to ensure that the right personnel and the right leadership are in place. They describe leadership practices that ensure hiring the right people with the right skills who embrace the philosophy and practices of inclusive education and who can work collaboratively with all stakeholders.

The importance of creating strong alliances with parents/guardians is discussed in Chapter 3, "*Forming a Necessary Partnership: Engaging the Families of Special Needs Students.*" More than ever, superintendents understand that leading a successful school district is directly linked to harnessing the support and assistance of all stakeholders, beginning with the families of the students.

The parents and guardians of special needs students must be involved in service and placement decisions for their child. Parent support of program placement is critical. School districts must find ways to engage parents positively and consistently. The coauthors of this chapter, Peter Davies and Christine N. Michael, are seasoned educators who offer practical insights to assist superintendents with building bridges to the parent community.

Chapter 4, "*Rethinking the Assignment of Paraprofessionals: Ensuring Students Are Well Served Within Budget Constraints,*" provides a method for hiring and utilizing paraprofessional staff. Due to the increased inclusion of special needs students in general education classes, the use of paraprofessionals has proliferated dramatically. Futures Education has developed a protocol that analyzes the current use of paraprofessionals and provides an effective and efficient guide for the design of service delivery and support. The chapter was written by Nicholas D. Young, PhD, a current superintendent in Massachusetts; Peter J. Bittel, the founder and chief executive officer of Futures Education; and Michael Neiman, PhD, a speech pathologist.

Special education expenditures frequently approach 20%–30% of a district's budget to meet the needs of only 10%–15% of the total student population. Chapter 5, "*Methods to Meet the Budget Challenges in Special Education,*" offers a practical guide to resource allocation for special education programs. This chapter provides information and advice to superintendents, demonstrating how vigilant oversight will promote increased efficiencies.

The legislative requirements of IDEA, NCLB, and Section 504 have had a significant impact on the delivery of related services. In chapter 6, "*NCLB and IDEA: Related Services and the Law,*" Erin Edwards, Peter J. Bittel, Michael Neiman, Herbert Levine, and Wendy C. Reed offer a guide to the ins and outs of the federal mandates. Practical legal insights will aid superintendents in better understanding districts' responsibilities regarding the provision of related services.

Chapter 7, "*Superintendents' Use of Special Education Data and Performance Measures in an Environment of Accountability,*" delves into the world of data and performance standards, worlds that not only are potentially overwhelming to superintendents, but also represent key indicators for which they are held accountable. A former business administrator and superintendent provide strategies for keeping data fluid and simple. This chapter provides a practical guide to data management, including a framework for data collection, and identifies the information critical to the oversight of special education delivery systems.

The book concludes with chapter 8, *"Special Education Transportation: Why It Is Expensive and What Can Be Done to Reduce the Cost."* Some have questioned the need for a separate chapter on transportation. The fact is that special education transportation expenses have grown at much faster rates than the rates of regular education transportation. Containing transportation costs for special education is vitally important. The framework and protocols in this chapter have been adopted and utilized in districts across the country, resulting both in significant savings and improved quality of service.

NOTES

1. According to the National Center for Educational Statistics, the United States spends over $800 billion on public education. The study noted that adjusted for inflation and parental fees (pay for play, field trip costs, dues and fees, lab fees) the cost exceeds $1 trillion.

2. Some researchers have stated that only 30% of inner city youth graduate from high school.

Chapter 1

The Superintendent's Role in Special Education Leadership

David Larson, PhD, Herbert Levine, PhD, Dominick C. Vita, PhD, and Nicholas D. Young, PhD, EdD

CURRENT STATE OF SPECIAL EDUCATION

Special education programming often constitutes 20%–30% of a school district's budget. The national average for special education prevalence in school districts is approximately 13% of a given district's total student population.

According to the National Education Association, the number of US students enrolled in special education programs has risen 30% over the last ten years. Three of every four students with disabilities spend part or all of their school day with their general education peers. Nearly every general education classroom across the country includes students with disabilities.

The conundrum facing the superintendent is how to both manage programs and create an environment in which decisions related to special education maximize the use of district resources and better meet the needs of all students. According to the US Department of Education, approximately $12.8 billion is spent each year for special education programming under the Individuals with Disabilities Education Act (IDEA) and No Child Left Behind (NCLB).

The federal government annually allocates an average of $1,750 per special education student. The balance of the costs for providing special education and related services is provided by local and state revenues.

Superintendents face complicated annual budget battles and often tend to play a hands-off role in the management of special education programs. It is not uncommon for superintendents to believe that the rising cost of special education programs is compromising general education programs. And superintendents, along with other stakeholders, often believe there is nothing they can do about special education due to legally mandated requirements.

Contrary to such common belief, superintendents can and must play a significant role in the planning, oversight, and management of special education programs and services. The success of special education programs and services is a shared responsibility. No longer can the superintendent leave this responsibility to others. Although the principal and the special education administrator may ultimately be responsible for the delivery of services, the superintendent will be held accountable by the local school board and the public at large.

The influence on special education services by the superintendent is critical. It is essential for the superintendent to have a general understanding of the basic operations and requirements of special education programs as well as the role and function of the special education leadership and the department as a whole. In turn, special education administrators must understand the superintendent's role in leading the entire district. The roles must be symbiotic and aligned.

The superintendent must define clear expectations for the district. The special educators must keep the superintendent informed and involved, promoting a culture of collaboration and accountability. A major game changer for assuring positive outcomes in special education programs and services is for the superintendent to be involved in analyzing achievement data, monitoring staffing costs, embracing the philosophy and practice of inclusive education, and fostering a culture of collaboration to achieve a collective sense of accountability between general and special education.

THE WORK: ORGANIZATIONAL CHANGES

Inherent tension occurs during the identification, implementation, and staffing of special education programs. Student identification practices and staffing decisions are often based at the school building level. When decisions are made at the school level, unless there is a clear and coherent culture of collaboration including common language and needs, special education management may become fragmented.

Drucker (2008) emphasizes the importance of culture in any organization. The superintendent must lead the development of a culture that breaks down the barriers often existing between general and special education. The superintendent needs to develop a collaborative culture promoting best practice in the interest of the student, not the adult. All involved must row together to maximize student achievement.

Special education has a unique set of mandates and nuances. According to the US Department of Education Budget for 2011, in addition to the more traditionally recognized school-age services, money is allocated for the following programs:

1. Preschool to elementary service and transition;
2. High school to post-secondary transition;
3. Career and vocational education;
4. Community living skills.

Local public school districts are responsible for providing special education and related services to identified students with disabilities ages three through twenty-one years of age.[1] According to the National Institute on Disability and Rehabilitation Research, schools play an important role not only in educational service delivery, but also in the delivery of rehabilitation services to students.

The effectiveness of schools is often determined by the results of standardized testing of students, including the performance of special education students. IDEA, as reauthorized in 1997, mandated that students with disabilities be included in state- and district-wide assessments.

Because NCLB requires comparisons that are often used as a media measure of a district's success, superintendents must pay particular attention to how the management of special education programs influences achievement data. The culture that a superintendent must foster is one of accountability and inclusion. Research shows that districts with a distinct separation between general education and special education have higher costs and less satisfactory student results. Districts that foster a culture with increased focus on inclusion and alignment with the general education curriculum had lower costs and better student outcomes.

Most general education teachers have little special education training, and even less training in supervising paraprofessionals assigned to their classrooms. Teachers often feel unprepared and overwhelmed with the responsibility of meeting the needs of students with diverse abilities, skills levels, and educational needs. In addition, special education students' test results may have a substantially negative impact on the statistical performance of the class as a whole on mandated performance assessments.

General education teachers now teach a wider spectrum of students with cognitive, academic, social, emotional, and physical disabilities. They are also expected to work collaboratively with other educators and specialists in the classroom providing related services such as speech, physical, and occupational therapy and other support services. New expectations and changes to the classroom structure can be supported and perfected through a comprehensive, job-embedded professional development program, proper supervision, and meaningful support with formative assessment for teachers.

The goal is to integrate general and special education to maximize the educational benefits for both general education students and students with special needs. This entails minimizing the separation of special end general education at all levels of program operations.

REDEFINING SPECIAL EDUCATION AS A SERVICE

Special education is a service, not a place. This conceptual change in understanding of service delivery created a focus on making sure that 80% of the students with disabilities are educated in the general education environment 80% of the time. The current expectation is that special education instruction and services are integrated into the general education environment, thereby providing an appropriate learning experience in the least restrictive environment (LRE).

This approach allows students with special needs to benefit from the enriched general education classroom and school environment with regular education peers. Collaborative design of programs and services, coupled with a more flexible model of cooperative staffing, will both promote student performance and maximize the effectiveness and efficiency of educational personnel.

The concepts and implementation of LRE and free appropriate public education (FAPE) must be clearly understood and implemented by all educators as the philosophical base for all learning activities in schools. The superintendent's role is pivotal to the development of a productive educational environment in which both educators and students can attain successful performance outcomes.

Superintendent Span of Control

Although it is essential that the superintendent remain involved with, and be aware of, the operation of special education programs and services, there should be no need to micromanage special education programs, services, or staff. Systemic policies, practices, and cultural processes need to be communicated effectively so the superintendent stays informed and engaged in special education programs. This will maximize the effectiveness and efficient implementation of all programs within the organization.

As mentioned earlier, the superintendent must create a culture that encourages information sharing, frequent data collection, and analysis. Relevant questions need to be asked by leadership to drive program decisions.

The superintendent needs to provide ongoing and frequent data sharing with the central office, general education, and special education staff in a collaborative yet precise manner.

PREREFFERAL PRACTICES: ACADEMIC AND BEHAVIOR ASSESSMENT, PROGRESS MONITORING, AND INTERVENTIONS

Prerefferal interventions are an essential component of the general education program. General education carries the responsibility for addressing the diverse educational needs of all students. Although the term "prerefferal" may be a misnomer because it implies that a referral to special education will follow, the concept of prerefferal refers to the intervention provided in the classroom by the teacher. It also refers to other supports available to assist students who are struggling or underperforming academically or behaviorally, in an effort to avert a referral to special education.

In many cases, the lack of adequate interventions and support in general education leads to frustration on the part of students, parents, teachers, and administrators. The frustration often results in a referral for special education testing and placement. The possibility of premature abandonment of responsibility by general education and associated supports should compel educators ethically to rethink the prevention of identifying a student as having a disability when, in fact, that student requires only supplemental general education instruction and support.

The superintendent can exert significant influence on the general education capacity of a school or district to meet the needs of students by insisting on a variety of prerefferal instructional interventions. Although response to intervention (RtI) and positive behavior supports are currently viewed as the most effective general education interventions, there are various strategies that will provide effective general education interventions for students not meeting expectations.

By far, the most effective strategy for minimizing an inappropriately high number of students assigned to special education programs and services is an expansion of the capacity of general education programs and the skills of regular education personnel to meet the educational needs of all students. Inappropriate identification will diminish only when students are provided with the supports and instructional opportunities that enable them to be successful in the regular classroom.

The high incidence of referrals to special education should be considered to be an indicator of deficiencies in the general education program. Differentiated instruction, classroom modifications, and instructional practices that address different student learning styles, needs, abilities, preferences, educational backgrounds, socioeconomic conditions, and home supports are all issues that can, and should, be addressed through enhancing the capacity of the general education program.

Frequent progress monitoring of academic outcomes and behavior in conjunction with data analysis related to progressive interventions enable professionals to make effective decisions that will have a positive impact on student performance, teacher performance, and organizational structures. This investment will require significant time and resources in engaging all staff in meaningful embedded professional development that targets the desired change.

Identification and Eligibility for Special Education Services

The prerefferal process serves as the process and policy for Child Find. It is the school district's responsibility to have procedures in place to ensure identification of students who have special needs and to provide free and appropriate public education responsive to the student's instructional requirements. Inevitably, there will be students identified as requiring special education and related services that have been provided appropriate general education support but still need additional support through special education services.

District-wide identification procedures must include clearly defined eligibility criteria and uniform application of evaluative practices by all educators and service providers. Consistent and appropriate procedures must also be in place to determine when a student no longer requires special education or related services.

In the majority of cases, the provision of special education services should yield observable benefits that enable a student to develop skills to perform successfully in the general education environment with a reduced level of support as the student progresses through the grade levels. This is a positive outcome for the district and student in that the student will have achieved the level of competency necessary to perform in general education at reduced levels of support and for the school to demonstrate accountability for successful services.

In-District and Out-of-District Programming

Depending upon the state and district, the issue of out-of-district (OOD) placements can be a substantial financial and programmatic challenge for school superintendents. Placements are defined in a variety of different terms throughout the country. Typically, an out-of-district educational placement is contracted with a private or public special education service provider. Funding for out-of-district placement varies from state to state.

Some placements are necessitated by circumstances such as serious physical or medical conditions, psychiatric conditions, or the existence of low incidence disabilities. Some disabilities require specialized services that are unavailable within the district. However, out-of-district placements can frequently be avoided by developing capacity within the district to provide appropriate special education instruction and related services.

As stated early in this chapter, special education is not a place. It is a range of services as specified in an individualized education program for a particular student who may be integrated within the general education organizational structure. An ongoing analysis of the types, frequency, and duration of student supports that result in out-of-district placements should be conducted to enable the district to develop and adjust its capacity to provide education for all students within the schools of the district, thereby meeting the requirements of FAPE.

Superintendents must spur the development of in-district school-based capacity to appropriately meet the needs of students who might otherwise be recommended for out-of-district placements. Effective in-district programming provides special education and related services to students with disabilities in the LRE with age-appropriate peers in the home school district. Effective in-district programs also save the district the significant cost of out-of-district placements, provide collaborative services to neighboring districts, and possibly generate tuition income.

Districts with effective specialized programs and services may wish to accept students from other districts, thereby providing additional revenues to a district and potentially mitigating some of the challenges of limited local funding. This strategy may supplement the district's budget while also minimizing the expense of transportation and tuition costs associated with out-of-district placements. A superintendent's leadership in monitoring programs and services opportunities will create more student placement flexibility while also being cost-effective for district program operations.

Data Needs: Keep it Simple

Due to the increased focus nationally on data-based decision making, and the heightened attentiveness to quantifying student performance, educators can become overloaded with data. Special educators are required to maintain copious records on each student and must meet federal and state data reporting requirements. Meaningful data can provide a superintendent and other educators with information that is essential in the decision making about programs and services. Ongoing communication should take place between the superintendent and the lead administrator of special education.

THE WORK: VALUES AND CLIMATE ENCULTURATION

Building Instructional Capacity and Leadership

In the final analysis, districts are judged on the improvement each student makes. Although NCLB, IDEA, and other state and federal reporting requirements hold districts and individual schools accountable, external measures may not address the true progress of a special education student. Special education is a general education challenge as it is a subsystem of the larger education system. Leadership that increases accountability for student achievement provides collaborative organizational structures, procedures, and processes for all stakeholders.

Special educators working collaboratively with classroom teachers create a student-centered climate. Individual student goals must be realistic, yet be consistent with external assessments. Ideally, the individualized education program (IEP) for each student will align with the district curriculum and reflect the state standards by which assessments will occur.

The more deliberate the focus on inclusion as a philosophy and educational approach, along with progress monitoring within the general education curriculum, the greater the opportunities are to increase the instructional capacity of all staff. Professional development, use of RtI, and the creation of a collaborative culture to meet the needs of students will enhance student success.

Albert Einstein said, "The definition of insanity is doing the same thing over and over again and expecting different results." In some cases, districts are forced to do things differently; however, the superintendent must be the catalyst for proactive and positive change in the leadership of special education.

According to the *InForum* (2009), "All of the superintendents must maintain a clear and consistent focus on student learning. Likewise, superintendents must have a clear belief based on personal and/or professional experiences that students benefit when general education and special education collaborate" (p. 7). In this report, several superintendents reported that collaboration between general and special educators enhanced all student performance. Identified strategies included

- Articulate clear and consistent goals and expectations;
- Provide extensive and ongoing professional development for all staff that supports the district's goals and expectations and fosters a dialogue among general education and special education;
- Focus on meeting the needs of all students, regardless of label;
- Maintain data management systems;

- Use student data to analyze student needs, make instructional decisions, and convince others of the need for collaboration between special educators and general educators;
- Be open and transparent about data;
- Start small;
- Hire the right personnel to implement this collaboration;
- Counsel out personnel who are not on board;
- Cultivate "buy-in" from all stakeholders;
- Maintain the focus at the district level, even though some decisions are made at the building level;
- Model the collaboration you wish to see at the building level;
- Organize and structure offices, personnel, and schedules that systemically sustain and support collaboration.

The focus on achievement in NCLB and IDEA has served as a catalyst for collaboration. Superintendents must demonstrate the leadership to bring collaboration to the forefront. Historically, special educators and general educators have operated within independent systems with a separate budget and isolated staffing decisions. As stated previously, special education is truly a general education challenge. The superintendent must promote, develop, and sustain a culture of collaboration between general and special educators.

NEXT STEPS

Data analysis and collaboration will enhance all students' learning. Superintendents must develop a culture of collaboration and maintain a systemic overview of all programs. Professional development will offer the superintendent, and other change agents, the opportunity to work with staff. Professional development should focus on collaboration, prereferral interventions such as RtI, and special education issues that will capture the attention of general educators.

Interdisciplinary professional development offers the opportunity for learning and collaboration. Superintendents need to lead the initiatives by encouraging all leaders in the district to adhere to best practices by expanding the continuum of services in special education to meet the needs of all students. Concurrently, the district must build its capacity to effectively educate students, with or without disabilities, in the general education environment.

The best education is specialized within the general education classroom, providing every student with learning experiences that are most effective when students and teachers share the experience. An integrated service model results in higher levels of achievement if students are provided differentiated instruction and other supports aligned with individual needs. In order to accomplish this, teachers and administrators should use professional learning communities (PLCs), prerefferal strategies such as RtI, common planning time, common assessments, and multiple intervention strategies to support student learning.

Another essential strategy is hiring individuals that have the right capabilities and enthusiasm along with an interactive spirit. There are many challenges in the delivery of services in a collaborative environment.

CONCLUSION

Systemic change requires investment by all stakeholders. Resistant staff create barriers if they feel that a change to the program threatens their job security. Often they do not recognize their role in the changes. The focus must remain on the student. As superintendent, it is important to ensure that the work is collaborative, thoughtful, caring, and directed toward outcomes that matter in the lives of the student.

It is a fallacy that superintendents can do nothing about special education delivery systems, and a fatal flaw to ignore the management of special education programs and services as they relate to the overall success of district performance. The development of a transparent system that merges rather than separates general education and special education is essential to build capacity and create an environment of inclusion for both students and staff.

Superintendents need to facilitate consistent and timely restructuring of programs and services, enhancing accessibility and building a strong but flexible organizational structure. The alignment of general education and special education strategies will provide a better educational experience for all students while simultaneously assuring responsible allocation of finite district human, fiscal, and pedagogical resources.

REFERENCES

Americans with Disabilities Act (ADA) of 1990, 42 U.S.C. Sections 12101–12213.
Drucker, P. (2008). *Classic Drucker.* Boston: Harvard Business School Press.
Individuals with Disabilities Education Act (IDEA), 20 U.S.C. § 1401 (a) (22).
Individuals with Disabilities Education Act (IDEA), 20 U.S.C. Implementing Regulations at 34 C.F.R. § 300.2 (15) (a), § 300.24 (b) (15), § 104.43, Section 104.37.
Keller-Allen, Chandra. "Superintendent Leadership: Promoting General and Special Education Collaboration." *InForum*, U.S. Department of Education. September, 2009.
National Institute on Disabilities and Rehabilitation. Institute on Disability and Rehabilitation Research, www.ed.gov/about/offices/list/osers/nidrr/index.html.
Rehabilitation Act of 1973, Section 504. United States Department of Education, http://www.ed.gov.

POINTS TO REMEMBER

Change and collaboration do not come naturally or easily. The challenges facing superintendents in the oversight of special education programs are many, and should necessitate the following actionable items:

- *Obtain consensus from staff and parents;*
- *Promote the district's vision to all stakeholder groups: work with special education parents and advocates to find common ground and to clearly define FAPE and LRE in order to meet needs of students with disabilities;*
- *Find the proper experts to provide embedded professional development;*
- *Create efficiencies in personnel scheduling and workloads;*
- *Understand that special education is really a general education challenge;*
- *Change pedagogy to meet the needs of all students with realistic instructional goals and objectives for all students that are quantifiable and verifiable;*
- *Create a collaborative environment so general education staff understand the instructional needs of special education students, and promote a collaborative spirit that outlines the strengths and weaknesses of the entire instructional program;*
- *Create valid and reliable site-specific documentation systems that support the needs of all students and ensure compliance;*
- *Create a valid system of internal accountability that goes beyond assessment;*
- *Build staff appreciation that special education services are ideally provided on a temporary basis with specific goals for declassification when appropriate;*
- *Promote an understanding of the prereferral process.*

NOTE

1. These ages may vary somewhat from state to state and actually may start as low as two years, six months of age and continue through age twenty-two or even twenty-six in some states. Early childhood (birth to age three) programs are also funded through various government sources. In some states, these programs are operated by the local school system.

Chapter 2

Organizational, Personnel, and Fiscal Considerations in the Oversight of Special Education Services

Brian Edwards, MEd, and Dominick C. Vita, PhD

THE WHO: ORGANIZATIONAL CAPACITY

The evolution of special education over the past four decades has resulted in varied administrative and organizational structures in school districts. Prior to the introduction of Public Law 94-142 and its seismic impact on special education, the most common organizational structure consisted of a chief administrator of pupil personnel services. The position was usually held by either a director or assistant superintendent of pupil personnel services.

Although guidance, social work, school health services, and other student support services were typically included within the organizational purview of pupil personnel services, special education generally constituted a relatively minor component of the overall structure. Many superintendents around the country subscribe to a philosophy of organizational leadership through the creation and maintenance of a learning organization.

In a learning organization, all departments within a school district work in concert as opposed to a "silo" practice of individual district departments operating in a vacuum. A learning organization reflects a philosophy and an attitude that views districts and the associated "actors" as efficacious and capable of exceptional performance even in the face of obstacles (Cameron, Dutton, and Quinn, 2003). Even so, many special education departments still operate very separately from other district operating units.

In the post 94-142 era, a greater number of students and subsequent resources are allocated into special education services. Special education programs have developed into a greater programmatic, operational, and fiscal component of the overall education delivery system in school districts. As a result, it is more important for superintendents to have a good understanding of the programs and services as well as open communication with the director.

Unless they have a background in special education, most superintendents do not have a comprehensive knowledge of the intricacies of related programming. Even if a superintendent has a strong relevant background, the demands of the role are such that one cannot, nor should it be necessary to, spend an inordinate amount of time focusing on special education issues. Therefore, the importance of finding the right administrator cannot be overstated.

Collins (2001) has suggested an analogy that likens the CEO of an organization to a bus driver. First, the driver must decide where he is going, how to get there, and who is going with him. Collins advises that it is most critical to first get the right people on the bus in the right "seats" and remove the wrong people from the bus. In the case of the superintendent as CEO, the superintendent should have a broad conception of the general requirements and vision for special education as part of the overall school district.

Collins deems it critical to start with the "who" rather than the "where." To continue the analogy of superintendent as CEO, hiring a director of special education[1] is the first step to creating a successful program. Whatever the reporting structure, the key to effective program delivery is the clarity of expectations for performance based on collaboration and effective use of data for decision making. The culture of collaboration drives the most effective delivery of services.

Procedural Considerations

The hiring process for a director of special education often involves a large committee that oversees the solicitation of applications, preliminary screening of candidates, interviews that may involve a cast of thousands, and ultimately the selection of an individual for the position. Although politically expedient, the limitation of a selection committee is that there is often not a clear and consistent definition of the type of professional who will be most effective.

Research supports the notion that successful recruiting methods demand strategies to address the operational challenges of the hiring process and, therefore, require a thorough and accurate understanding of the characteristics of the special education director (Borman and Dowling, 2008). In order to design a strong selection process, a representative from each stakeholder group (e.g., parents, special education and general education teachers, board members) may be a part of the selection committee with the superintendent's or designee's guidance. Because the superintendent will ultimately be held accountable for the performance and success of the program, the hiring of the director of special education should reside with the superintendent.

There are numerous organizational structures and titles for the administration of special education instruction. There may also be multiple layers of administrators, and other leadership positions, depending upon the size of the district. Chief special education administrative positions may be designated as assistant superintendents. If so, the administrator will typically oversee all special education and related services as well as the traditional pupil personnel services.

In addition to the director of special education, many districts also employ supervisory administrators of special education. Supervisors, although an integral part of the total leadership team, tend to be program or school based and are expected to manage the day-to-day activities in schools pertaining to special education and related services.

Another common organizational scenario has the director of special education reporting to the chief administrator for curriculum and instruction. Some districts are organized in a manner that includes the director of special education in the superintendent's cabinet, whereas others are not.

Cultural Considerations

Regardless of the model, superintendents should be cognizant of any hint of symbolic or practical separation between general and special education. Such separation leads to the dreaded silo effect, creating an unintended void between general and special education.

It is important to keep in mind that the most effective special education service delivery model, with few exceptions, is in the general education classroom. It is preferable to promote a strong partnership that allows general education students to benefit from the strategy expertise of special educators and the special education students to simultaneously benefit from the content expertise of the general education staff.

Strategic leadership from the superintendent comes into play here. Leadership may be constrained by the inner environment, but strategic leaders can also affect and shape aspects such as the district's culture, strategy, and structure (Bass, 1998). Only through strong leadership from the superintendent can this philosophy of partnership between special educators and general educators be fostered.

Many superintendents tend to avoid direct involvement with special education because they might have limited knowledge or expertise in this area or they may perceive the program is only one of many district programs and is adequately supervised by the director. This laissez-faire approach is risky and often leads to problems—the more removed the director of special education is from the superintendent, the more inconsistent the special education program might be with the vision of the superintendent and the mission of the district.

Ongoing and meaningful communication regarding efficiencies, effectiveness, best practices, problems, and a myriad of other issues between the superintendent and the director is imperative. Because special education is such a complex domain requiring intensive collaboration, it is critical that channels of communication between the superintendent and the director of special education be open, systematic, consistent, and frequent.

PERSONNEL CAPACITY: WEARING MANY "HATS"

The multiple functions managed within the special education program form quite a lengthy list including

1. Academic instruction in all subjects;
2. Transportation schedules for students with disabilities;
3. Student assessment;
4. Personnel issues;
5. Grant writing;
6. Budget management and cost allocation;
7. Purchasing;
8. Program planning;
9. Due process mediations and hearings;
10. Litigation;
11. Source of information for school- and district-wide parent organizations;
12. Professional development;
13. Discipline issues;
14. Clinical practices related to psychology, speech-language, occupational therapy, physical therapy, and medical-related services;
15. Communication with state and other agencies;
16. District adherence to state and federal requirements, policies, procedures, and laws.

By necessity, the director of special education and other special education leadership personnel must be knowledgeable about a number of issues, practices, and procedures. When seeking a director of special education, superintendents should look for an individual who has a solid working knowledge of the aforementioned functions as well as federal and state special education laws and requirements. An effective director will understand the range of students with educational disabilities, as well as best practices for providing appropriate educational services in a cost-effective manner for programs supporting students from prekindergarten through post-secondary transition.

Management Ability

Depending upon the size and organization of the school district, the director of special education may or may not have direct supervisory responsibilities for classroom teachers and other school-based personnel. Regardless, the director must work closely with other supervisory personnel and school principals to ensure that all staff are performing their duties effectively and consistently within the parameters of each student's individualized education program (IEP). One of the most frequent difficulties in special education occurs when a program deviates from the prescribed specifications of an IEP. Supervisors provide support and monitoring to prevent deviation.

Staff and student schedules enable the efficient deployment of special education and related services. Inefficient school schedules developed without attention to special education needs adversely affect the efficient delivery of special education and related clinical services, and have a negative impact on the financial resources of a district. Special education administrators need to ensure the equity and continuity of recommended services from school to school and student to student. The director of special education, special education supervisors, principals, coordinators, teachers, and other service providers must work collaboratively to ensure schedules and services are being provided efficiently.

Effective Communication

The director should also be knowledgeable of general and special education laws, practices, and procedures. The effective director must be an excellent communicator, able to converse with a variety of school and community stakeholders. A strong skill set for any administrator includes the ability to facilitate compromise, to mediate differences, and to work cooperatively with various constituents to meet the needs of a broad range of interests. An effective special education administrator must also supervise administrative, office, and other staff, and serve as a positive member of the administrative team and of the larger educational community.

Special education leaders must also operationally define and enforce criteria that ensure all students have access to an appropriate education. The *appropriate* in *free appropriate public* education is one of the most ambiguous, and hence contentious, elements at the IEP meeting.

Often, a district's perspective of appropriate education is at odds with that of others involved in service planning for an individual student. Communication and decision making, based upon solid data and knowledge of effective practices, provide the entire IEP team with facts to collaboratively identify what special education services are appropriate—and what services are not.

DATA COLLECTION, ANALYSIS, AND IMPACT ON EFFECTIVE COMMUNICATIONS

Dealing with unhappy parents, aggressive advocates, attorneys, and others who may be presenting unrealistic demands is decidedly uncomfortable. The special education administrator must, in a professional manner, communicate with all involved without the use of intimidation. Districts cannot accede to pressure resulting in the provision of unnecessary services. The special education administrator must remain reasonable in negotiating a service plan in the best interests of both the district and the student.

The superintendent and director should be informed of prior conflicts, and view the problems collectively as learning experiences. Planning and preparation for meetings with relevant data is essential to keeping the focus on student achievement and needs. Ineffective or inappropriate special education services, poor parental relationships, breakdowns in school-home communication, and failure to adhere to or adjust the IEP to provide meaningful educational benefit are but a few of the many causes of litigation and due process hearings. Often disagreements leading to mediation or litigation can be diffused, resolved, and avoided long before the actual legal proceedings begin.

Parents satisfied with their student's program tend to avoid litigation or conflict with the district. The director of special education and other administrative and teaching personnel can avoid the expense and angst of such proceedings by ensuring services are provided as specified in the IEP and by addressing concerns before they become major problems. Problems are avoided through good communication, relationship building, and proper monitoring of service delivery and attention to the data on student achievement.

The Need for Support

The director of special education serves as the gatekeeper of the district's finite resources, while simultaneously striving for good relationships with everyone involved. The director may need to make difficult administrative decisions viewed as inconsistent with the expectations of parents, as well as staff and administration. Superintendents should recognize the possible dilemma, providing counsel and support for the director. The director and superintendent would be wise to share pertinent data supporting their decisions with stakeholders on a regular basis.

A critical skill for a director of special education is developing an understanding of the special education budget and the impact the budget has on the delivery of appropriate special education services to students. After decades of steady increases in revenues and expenses, public education now faces funding at a lower level than expenses. The numbers are staggering. More than half of the states in this country are facing significant revenue shortfalls in the immediate future (McNichol and Johnson, 2010).

The special education director must recognize the financial impact that a funding reduction of such magnitude will have on the special education budget, and deploy resources accordingly. Superintendents and business managers have experience in facing the challenges of reduced spending, while continuing to deliver appropriate educational services to students. The special education director should look to the superintendent and business manager for counsel, support, reporting methodologies, and help in problem-solving budget issues.

Creative Programming

Special education directors, in conjunction with district leadership, can be creative and entrepreneurial in the provision of services. For example, many school districts partner with private vendors to purchase services such as school maintenance, transportation, food services, substitute teacher employment and coordination, groundskeeping, health services, technology, legal services, security, and out-of-district special education placements.

Depending upon the size, location, and specific capacities of the district, contracted services can offer cost-effective alternatives to district employees, and to the purchase of equipment, utilities, management, clinical services, and other functions. Taking advantage of their purchasing power and their volume in conjunction with other districts, school systems can obtain better pricing for purchased services.

Innovative districts are also partnering with private and public companies to provide portions of special education instructional and related services such as speech and language therapy, occupational therapy, physical therapy, psychological services, and behavioral services.

Other new approaches such as teacher assistants, school-to-work transition, summer school, extended day or school year, special transportation, transportation management, and targeted professional development may also be considered for contracted services. Many districts benefit from partnering with a private company for a special education management contracting relationship wherein a private provider manages special education services for a district in lieu of the district having to employ a director of special education or supervisor of a particular special education service area.

CONCLUSION

The director of special education provides the leadership necessary to ensure the programmatic and fiscal integrity of special education programs and services. To do so, the director needs the consistent support of the superintendent. The once-held belief that the effectiveness and efficiency of special education are mutually exclusive constructs is not only false but also potentially destructive to the fiscal viability of an entire district. Financially sound solutions and excellent programming can be accomplished when leadership embraces a culture of collaboration and understanding of best practices and the educational laws that govern operations.

REFERENCES

Bass, B. M. (1998). *Transformational Leadership: Industry, Military, and Educational Impact.* Newark, NJ: Lawrence Erlbaum Associates.

Borman, G. D., and N. M. Dowling (2008). "Teacher Attrition and Retention: A Meta-Analytic and Narrative Review of the Research." *Review of Educational Research*, 78, 367–411.

Cameron, K. S., J. E. Dutton, and R. Quinn., eds. (2003). *Positive Organizational Scholarship.* San Francisco: Berrett-Koehler Publishers.

Collins, J. (2001). *Good to Great.* New York: HarperCollins.

McNichol, E., and N. Johnson (2010). *Recession Continues to Batter State Budgets: State Responses Could Slow Recovery.* Center on Budget and Policy Priorities, www.cbpp.org/cms/index.

POINTS TO REMEMBER

- *The organizational structure of the department responsible for special education should be compatible with the needs and organizational model of the district.*
- *Selecting effective administrators and leaders whose vision and capacities are aligned with that of the district is essential.*
- *Special education leaders must be cognizant of general education structure and issues, and be proactive in collaborating with leaders in this area.*
- *General education leaders must also be knowledgeable about special education and work cooperatively with special educators to provide effective and efficient programs and services aligned to free appropriate public education (FAPE) and least restrictive environment (LRE).*

- *The lines of communication between the superintendent and the leadership of special education must be established and maintained in an effective manner.*
- *Throughout the district, both general and special education programs must build a shared capacity to educate students with special needs.*

NOTE

1. Hereafter, this position shall be referred as the director of special education. There are, however, many titles (assistant superintendent, executive director, director, administrator, supervisor, coordinator, etc.) that various districts may use to designate this role.

Chapter 3

Forming a Necessary Partnership

*Engaging the Families of Special Needs Students -
An International Perspective*

Peter Davies, MA, and Christine N. Michael, PhD

In mainstream education there has been significant research over the last fifteen years about how family engagement advances achievement at school. Parental involvement has a significant positive effect on children's achievement and adjustment even after other factors shaping achievement have been removed from the equation. In early childhood education, the impact of parental involvement is even more important than variations in the quality of schools.

The research finding is consistent across all social classes and ethnic groups (Desforges and Abouchaar, 2003). Yet the evidence suggests that most families are not particularly engaged—and certainly not with their children's learning and schooling on a daily basis. Parents who represent populations that have long been marginalized by the majority culture are even less likely to be involved with the schools. Lack of family engagement—particularly at the secondary school level—is a constant challenge in most school districts.

Parents of children with special educational needs, however, often come to the school with a deep understanding of their child and a vital need for meaningful engagement. Many schools, running to keep pace with the increasing demands of high-stakes testing, budgetary constraints, unfunded mandates, and increasing accountability to the public fail to find time or lack the experience to engage with these parents. The irony is that they are likely the parents who know their children better than most, and who are open to productive engagement about their development and learning. From them there is much to be learned about parental engagement with learning.

There is indeed much to be learned in this era of increasingly complex definitions of family. The authors of this chapter acknowledge that in some instances it is a parent or parents who are key stakeholders in a child's education, and in others, families may consist of non-related individuals as primary caregivers who act in lieu of traditional parents. The transformative superintendent will recognize the often-missed opportunities for collaboration with nontraditional caregivers and stakeholders and the possibilities inherent in a new paradigm of family-school interaction.

FAMILY ENGAGEMENT: CROSS-CULTURAL VIEWS

Parents are *ipso facto* concerned about their children's well-being and wish for their children to be well, broadly, and fully educated to lead successful and prosperous lives. This holds true across cultures, regardless of the material and social context. From this perspective emerges a hierarchy of parental engagement with their growing children: the first level of engagement is in their physical well-being, the second level of engagement is in education and learning. Conceptually, the prioritized levels of engagement parallel Maslow's hierarchy of needs (1968) describing human psychological development.

The first level of parent engagement is a concern across all cultures and in all families. It encompasses the safety and well-being of children at all levels. Traditionally, for mothers, this requires health rituals and caring for sick or handicapped children. For fathers, the tasks tend to be focused on assuring sufficient family income. When there are sick children in the household it also may include raising funds for treatment.

The second level of parental engagement is engagement in education. This is more complex to describe, especially across cultures with sometimes starkly contrasting educational values. One common thread globally seems to be that parents and families first determine the "access points" to children's learning and then go about the tasks of enabling it.

Access points vary widely from class to class and culture to culture, and three examples from starkly different cultures follow. In Kenya and throughout East Africa, families (mainly mothers) take part in "Harambee"[1] savings clubs to meet a small fee tariff to educate their children at the neighborhood school that is perceived to be better than the government school.

In England, professional families, where both adults work long hours, arrange elaborate care arrangements for preschool children, often including a mixture of grandparental care,[2] paid care, and preschool or play group attendance.

For the Netsilik Eskimo of northern Canada, education means an early apprenticeship in fishing and hunting. Boys as young as four years will spend long hours away from the tribe with their fathers (Bruner, 1965).

In his recent book *The Social Animal: The Hidden Sources of Love, Character, and Achievement,* Brooks (2012) suggests an important relationship between the fundamental experiences of family learning and schooling. Brooks theorizes that the more institutionalized education becomes the more parents become estranged from their children's learning.

Over time schools have developed an awareness of this phenomenon, which has given rise to the efforts of involving parents through parent-teacher associations (PTAs), parent-teacher organizations (PTOs), and voluntary activities. Ironically and frequently, these now well-established methods that schools employ to *involve* parents become barriers to deeper and more critical parental *engagement* in their children's learning. In too many schools, the PTA becomes an elite, unrepresentative sampling of the wider parent group, and parents who are different, particularly minorities or non-English speakers, become increasingly marginalized.

FAMILY ENGAGEMENT: THE RESEARCH PERSPECTIVE

In a thought-provoking *Teachers College Record* article, Jeynes (2010), a professor at California State University, argues that while traditional forms of parent involvement are important (attending school functions, checking homework, enforcing rules about how children spend their leisure time), there are more subtle, holistic kinds of involvement at home—parental expectations, parent-child-school communication, and parental style—that are more important to student achievement.

As children grow to adolescence, the more this involvement can engage the school's agenda and vice versa the better. Jeynes also refers to a growing body of research suggesting a strong correlation between parental engagement in learning, particularly at home, and student achievement.

The correlation between family engagement and student achievement is further analyzed in the report *A New Wave of Evidence: The Impact of School, Family, and Community Connections on Student Achievement* (Henderson and Mapp, 2002). The researchers analyzed studies of high-achieving students from all backgrounds and found that their parents display a set of behaviors that develop and nurture their achievement. These parents encourage their children. They frequently talk with them about school, assist them in creating a post-secondary plan for higher education, and focus them regularly on their learning and homework assignments.

In 2003, Desforges and Abouchaar were commissioned by the United Kingdom's Department for Education and Skills (UK DfES, now DfE) to conduct a review of English language literature to establish research findings on the relationship between parental involvement, parental support, and family education on pupil achievement and adjustment in schools. The results provide an important synthesis of research demonstrating clear connections between family engagement in learning and student achievement.

Harris and Goodall, in their 2007 report commissioned by the same institution, found that the correlation between family engagement and raising student achievement becomes the cardinal point in their executive summary:

> Parental engagement is a powerful lever for raising achievement in schools. Where parents and teachers work together to improve learning, the gains in achievement are significant.

STARTING WITH STATUTES

In the United States, as in most mature Western economies, there are statutory requirements that mandate parents' engagement with schools. The statutory obligations, not surprisingly, have spawned considerable growth in organizations to encourage parental involvement in school programs. Parent councils in schools, parent information and resource centers (PIRCs), and regional education laboratories (RELs), federally funded by the US Department of Education, are a few such examples. Nationally and locally governed initiatives are a feature of parental engagement and involvement in Japan, Canada, and the United Kingdom.

Nationally funded initiatives in Japan, such as the National Institute for Educational Research, promote the utilization of conferences and home education to increase parental engagement and involvement. In Canada, parental engagement is embedded within school governance activities. The policy-making community at the provincial level is also largely concerned with the role of parents in school governance.

Similarly, members of the British school system's school governing bodies are elected, and these bodies often include parents. The Japanese model emphasizes the mediating role of teachers for the promotion of parental engagement and involvement. In Canada, the agenda has shifted to allow greater autonomy to schools relative to the involvement of parents.

FROM COMPLIANCE TO COLLABORATION

In the above global examples, there are also differences in statutes surrounding the roles of family and school in special education. A much-needed transformational approach to special education leadership entails moving from mere compliance with laws and mandates to respectful collaboration with families of special needs students.

Norway provides a useful example of a country responsive to the need to review and reassess the statutory/family relationship. In Norway, the National Support System for Special Needs Education (Statped) is managed by the Norwegian Directorate for Education and Training. Very recent Norwegian legislation reinforces the importance of the school-parent-child compact and paves the way for further advocacy and legislation. Parents receive specific information about the rights of their children, and their rights of lodging a complaint if they have doubts or disagree with authorities on whether these rights are being met in an adequate manner.

Norway also has standing committees such as the National Parents' Committee for Kindergartens and the National Parents' Committee for Primary and Lower Secondary Education that provide essential input into parent-school initiatives. Norwegian parents are provided with training and education to increase their ability to access and understand relevant educational information and advocate on their children's behalf.

Another Scandinavian example illustrates the impact of transformational leadership on school culture in Finland. It is hard to imagine the child with special educational needs, or his or her family, being blindsided by confusion within such a system. In classes rarely larger than twenty-four students, and with generous definitions of special educational needs, the push for quality is driven by quietly lifting all children up from the bottom, one at a time, through knowing them well in small classes, having specialist support at the point of learning, and not having to deal with excessive paperwork and endless external initiatives.

A transformational culture is particularly important for older students with special educational needs. High school students with learning disabilities or emotional and behavioral disorders are more likely than others to experience depression, anxiety, conduct problems, delinquency, school dropout, incarceration, and poor outcomes after they leave school. As the example below indicates, family engagement drops off significantly as students move through their school years.

In a presentation for Centre for Real-World Learning, Bill Lucas cites Sacker (2002), offering a simple but rich data analysis of the changing need for family engagement over time. A seven-year-old derives 29% of the impact on his/her academic achievement from parenting and 5% from schooling; the figures shift to 27% and 21% respectively at age eleven, and 14%

and 51% at age sixteen. The figures reinforce the importance of parents finding ways to stay engaged with their children and suggest that schools at all levels need to recognize the complex professional messages behind the statistics.

PARENTAL INVOLVEMENT VERSUS PARENTAL ENGAGEMENT

Although the terms *involvement* and *engagement* are often used interchangeably when referencing school-family interactions, there is a difference between the two. *Merriam-Webster's Dictionary* defines the first as being enfolded or enveloped, with the latter as being interlocked with or enmeshed. The definitional differences in practice mean that involvement may presume or subsume the families' beliefs and wishes, while engagement tends to elicit these, and other valuable information, from the families.

Too often, families are forced to become involved with the school system as a result of mandates, laws, and even behavioral issues. Their involvement is dictated by the school and other agencies, and it may be accompanied by a sense of fear, confusion, anger, or shame. While the savvy superintendent certainly needs to promote family involvement, there is a higher level of productive participation when families are positively engaged.

FAMILY AND PARENT ENGAGEMENT INITIATIVES

Many parent engagement initiatives place a particular focus on educational reform by way of parental advocacy. Such initiatives exist in the United States, the United Kingdom, and Canada, with examples such as the Parent Educational Advocacy Training Center in the United States, the Family and Parenting Institute in the United Kingdom, and Safe and Healthy Schools in Canada, an organization that grew out of advocating for school safety but has now become a network of associated companies and non-governmental organizations (NGOs) offering a breadth of parent engagement resources.

For most initiatives the implicit or explicit mission is to make the best of institutionalized schooling by advocating for students' educational rights. Many of the organizations have a focus on special educational needs, second language, or minorities' issues. Unfortunately, the majority of parent engagement initiatives still place parents in the position of having to initiate contact with parental engagement professionals within institutions, therefore placing less of an emphasis on the teachers, educators, and administrators to reach out to parents and the community.

When parent liaison personnel are employed, as they are in a number of school districts in the United States and schools in the United Kingdom, they often become the sole point of contact; the real engagement of the parent at the point of learning often remains lost.

WHAT WORKS

A Clear and Consistent Vision

In chapter 1 of this book, the authors make the case for the superintendent's role clearly defining the expectations of the district and fostering a culture of collaboration to achieve a collective sense of accountability between general and special education. The superintendent is responsible for inspiring his/her district(s) to attain equity and achievement.

In his book on eliminating "ableism," Hehir (2011) rails against the dumbing down of the curriculum that, he believes, occurs when schools pay too much attention to student deficits and not enough to maximizing opportunities for using the capabilities that special students possess. He feels such an orientation deprives special students of an equitable chance to participate in society. He concludes that the key is positive, consistent strategies for dealing with behavior and learning interventions for all students, and that sound strategies for all lead to higher achievement for all.

Creating the Critical Climate

Murray and Pianta (2007) suggest a number of areas for transformational reform that benefit all students, but that are especially helpful for students with special needs. They argue that the most effective learning culture is authoritative, warm, and demanding. Other studies have found that the key components of an effective educational culture are high expectations for achievement, consistent praise and feedback, personal involvement, and strong classroom management and discipline policies. Research also supports the effectiveness of regular one-on-one meetings with students and parents to set goals and monitor progress.

Educating and Supporting Staff

While most teachers and educational staff have been required to have substantial exposure to information and mandates involving special needs students and their families, they may not have experienced the power of hearing the stories and learning from such students and their families. Whenever possible and appropriate, balancing the technical side of special education with the personal can promote greater two-way understanding and trust.

Staff who engage in regular communication, collaboration, and creative problem solving with families of special needs students frequently experience stress and burn out, as the aforementioned are extremely time-consuming activities. Superintendents must acknowledge the value of this approach and provide ample time and support for it to occur.

The Relational Role of Family Engagement

Engaging families of special needs students requires building genuine relationships; relationship building begins with creating a dialogue that recognizes that the families of special needs children have dreams for their children, just as all families do. Successful engagement also honors the principle that families are a rich repository of knowledge about their child as a learner and that this knowledge must be tapped, rather than being seen as interfering with school-driven initiatives.

Developing a trusting, reciprocal relationship means that school staff must accept that some families will initially present with denial, anger, shame, or culturally different definitions of special needs, and that it may be a lengthy process to arrive at a true, equitable relationship. Through the Parent Teacher Home Visit Project in Sacramento and the Industrial Areas Foundation in Texas and other parts of the United States, engaging families always begins with a home visit to elicit the family's hopes, dreams, values, and beliefs in relation to their special needs student.

A Level Playing Field

Successful schools will understand, immediately, that no family engagement undertakings will work unless real-life barriers to participation are removed or minimized. Time, cost, transportation, child care, language barriers, lack of technology, and level of parental education are but a few of the roadblocks to full engagement. Special education family members are the best source of creative problem solving when it comes to planning activities that eliminate or lessen many of the potential pitfalls.

At the Luther Burbank High School in Sacramento, Ferlazzo (2009) reports on an internationally recognized family literacy project that provides computers and Internet access at home to families who needed them. This happened only after parents suggested the idea, reached out to organize other parents, and worked alongside teachers to articulate an implementation plan.

Equal Opportunity

Special students and their families also need parity when it comes to participation in co-curricular activities. Too often, special needs students are not given opportunities to be mentors, athletes, or leaders in their school and community, or participants in forms of community service. Dr. Virginia Wilkins, a national expert on mentoring in US schools, sees the effect that such co-curricular activities have.

At Delta Opportunity School in Colorado, a last-chance alternative high school in which many students have learning differences, high school students mentor special needs students at a local preschool, as well as run the award-winning Food for Thought program that provides backpacks filled with nutritious meals for families that otherwise would go hungry when school meals are not provided. Winning the county's Community Service Award raised the esteem of students and their families and gave them new status in the eyes of the community.

At Landmark College in Vermont, special needs students and their families are invited for a college day. One of the highlights of the day, says Wilkins (2012), "is the panel where college students talk about their special needs, their medication, and tell their stories so that the younger students learn that they, too, can go to college." Further, she notes, "often it is the parents who become most excited when they realize that their children are 'college material' and this increases their involvement in school."

Celebrating Success

As special needs students and their families are better integrated into the full life of the school, there will be more opportunities for celebrating student success. Left out of the mainstream athletic, academic, and leadership recognitions in the past in most schools, special students can take more prominent roles in awards and celebrations when schools adopt a more inclusive view of achievement, leadership, and service.

Parents as Co-Creators of Knowledge and Planning

Elaine Mulligan, veteran special education teacher and current project coordinator for the Urban Schools Improvement Program at Arizona State University, notes, "It's easy for teachers to get into the habit of thinking of parents as nuisances or even the enemy." This attitude can be exacerbated by an often contentious and litigious special education landscape (McLaughlin, 2007).

In including family members as a part of the individualized education program (IEP) process, "there is an understanding that parents of an exceptional child have expertise in their child's specific learning needs." Mulligan recommends that educators listen to parents, consider their ideas, and utilize applicable feedback: "When that happens, the power dynamic is broken, and the 'us and them' mindset moves to a 'we' mindset."

Community Connections

In Lincoln, Nebraska, community groups came together in 2001 to form the Lincoln Learning Centers, providing academic support for struggling and talented learners, parent engagement opportunities, early childhood programs, counseling, career development, and lifelong learning. A transformational change took place in the community and school, not solely because of the activities themselves, but because they came from a community compact inspired by the idea that education is a community-wide responsibility.

Constant Communication

When teachers call each parent of the children in their class every week (as they do at Southside Academy Charter School in Syracuse, New York) it is often no more than a quick greeting—the total time burden is no more than an hour—but the connection reinforces relationships and permits discussion of any perceived issues before they escalate.

Secondary School Support

SEDL, the former Southwest Educational Development Laboratory in Texas, provides information on schools with promising practices. In one report, five high schools that have been particularly successful in engaging parents in their children's senior years of schooling are examined. Examples of good practice become fewer the older the students become, especially for students with special educational needs.

Characteristics common to the five successful schools in the study are strong communication protocols; collaborative activities with teachers around student learning; respecting home as the first and continuing learning environment; informal opportunities to chat; regular audits of parental satisfaction; and access for parents to be learners as well. Parents report feeling less and less capable of helping with their children's homework as they move into secondary-level courses, necessitating parent training in course content and use of technology if family members are to remain engaged in this role.

Families Mentoring Families

Since many families of children with special needs may have had less-than-positive school experiences themselves, they may feel more comfortable, at least initially, being formally or informally mentored by other families. This may entail having formal mentoring programs at transitional points in children's education such as entering kindergarten, middle school, or ninth grade; establishing groups that share language and cultural heritage, such as new immigrants or English language learners (ELLs); or having parents volunteer to staff a family resource center at school or in the community.

When family members have specific knowledge of disabling conditions and successful strategies that they have employed to address them, they can be invited to lead discussions or workshops with other families and staff.

Parent Academies

A successful example of the academy concept is the Logan Street Project in Chicago that is built on a full combination of learning about parenting, contributing to the work of the school, and engaging in self-improvement academically. Susan Zeig's documentary *A Community Concern* provides a good overview of some of this work, focusing on the Bronx, Boston, and Oakland.

Good examples of academies that integrate learning about parenting and parents as part of the learning agency for students are the Parent University in Boston and the Community Leadership Center at Rutgers-Camden in New Jersey. The latter also offers a parenting curriculum leading to certification.

The Camden Center's most notable project has been the multimillion-dollar Rutgers/LEAP Initiative, a comprehensive effort by Rutgers (the state university branch in Camden), to improve opportunities for children and families that involved creating the LEAP Academy University Public Charter School in 1997. Since then, all five of LEAP's graduating classes have achieved 100% college acceptance.

Rich Resources

In this age of information technology, there are many resources that aid the families of special needs students in gaining and sharing research and personal experience. A school parent resource center can provide computer access, assistance, and advocacy by helping families find what they need. Most parent engagement advocacy initiatives are not-for-profit organizations.

Initiatives vary in size from myriad homespun advocacy groups to the Harvard Family Research Project, the US National PTA (which dates back to 1897), and PTA-UK. These are some of the most proactive examples that produce a range of useful resources as well as established support networks.

Many of the smaller, activist-led organizations serve particular populations, such as minority groups, single-parent households, and parents of students with disabilities. Almost all the initiatives publish websites that provide resources. The aggregate of learning resources for parents who want to engage with their children is becoming a vast knowledge bank.

This knowledge bank incorporates various forms of multimedia including webinars, online leadership trainings, online classes/quizzes, informational booklets, pamphlets, toolkits, and articles. Access to these resources clearly increases exponentially with digital innovations. Literally tens of thousands of websites and hand-held applications are targeted at parents, but many parents may need the school's help in learning to employ them.

CONCLUSION

Advocating for parent and family engagement in schools has been and continues to be the work of people who by nature think inclusively. It is important that in reinforcing the essential importance of engaging with families of children with special educational needs one must respect and embrace this inclusive thinking to avoid producing yet further special, and often separate, arrangements.

The journey to achievement for all is one of including all families and all children in the development of strategies to promote meaningful learning in school including social and attitudinal learning, as well as academic achievement.

The effective superintendent will acknowledge that the school reform agenda needs to be revisited to encompass the widest possible group of stakeholders if true transformation is to occur. Within the group, the broader the representation of families and friends of children with wide-ranging special needs, the richer the outcome.

REFERENCES

Brooks, D. (2012). *The Social Animal: The Hidden Sources of Love, Character, and Achievement*. New York: Random House.

Desforges, C., and A. Abouchaar (2003). "The Impact of Parental Involvement, Parental Support, and Family Education on Pupil Achievement and Adjustment: Research Report 433." London: Department for Education and Skills, http://www.bgfl.org/bgfl/custom/files_uploaded_resources/18617/Desforges.pdf.

Ferlazzo, L. (2009). "Parent Involvement or Parent Engagement?" Learning First Alliance, May 9, 2009, http://www.learningfirst.org/LarryFerlazzoParentEngagement.

Harris, A., and J. Goodall (2007). "Engaging Parents in Raising Achievement: Do Parents Know They Matter?" Research Report DCSF-RW004. University of Warwick, http://wiki.ict-register.net/images/0/0a/July07Everyparentmatters.pdf.

Hehir, T. (2011). *New Directions in Special Education: Eliminating Ableism in Policy and Practice*. Cambridge, MA: Harvard Education Press.

Henderson, A. T., and K. L. Mapp (2002). *A New Wave of Evidence: The Impact of School, Family, and Community Connections on Student Achievement*. National Center for Family & Community Connections with Schools. Austin, TX: Southwest Educational Development Laboratory.

Jeynes, W. (2010). "The Salience of the Subtle Aspects of Parental Involvement and Encouraging That Involvement: Implications for School-Based Programs." *Teachers College Record*, 112, no. 3: 747–774.

McLaughlin, Laurie. (2007). "Modeling the Parent-Teacher Strategies of Special Education." National Education Association, http://www.nea.org/home/16265.htm.

Maslow, A. H. (1968). *Toward a Psychology of Being.* 2nd ed. Princeton, NJ: Van Nostrand Reinhold.

Murray, C., and R. Pianta (2007). "The Importance of Teacher-Student Relationships in Adolescents with High Incidence Disabilities." *Theory into Practice*, 46, no. 2.

Sacker, A., I. Schoon, and M. Bartley (2002). "Social Inequality in Educational Achievement and Psychological Adjustment throughout Childhood: Magnitude and Mechanisms." *Social Studies and Medicine*, 55, 863–880.

Unpublished interview. Wilkins, Virginia. Interview by Christine Michael. Professional. Manchester, Vermont, February 22, 2012.

POINTS TO REMEMBER

Engaging parents of special children is a critical, but complex, undertaking. In transforming the relationship between family and school, superintendents should consider the following recommendations:

- *Recognize the difference between involvement and engagement.*
- *Create an ongoing process of assessing parents' perceived needs, interests, and wishes in relation to their children's education.*
- *Be aware of the barriers that prevent parental engagement such as time, cost, transportation, child care, language spoken at home, lack of technology, and level of parent education and plan concrete strategies to eliminate or minimize them.*
- *Provide opportunities for families to learn alongside their children and adolescents, especially when new curricula and new uses of technology are involved.*
- *Dedicate time and resources to educating and coaching/mentoring faculty and staff on ways to promote family engagement.*
- *Honor the principle that the transfer of knowledge and cultural understanding must flow equally from school to family and family to school by creating opportunities for families to provide expertise to the school community.*
- *Provide equitable co-curricular opportunities for special needs students and their families and celebrate their successes in these venues.*
- *Tap the rich resources of the community to support special needs families.*
- *Strategize with families to prevent the drop-off of family involvement in secondary school initiatives.*

NOTES

1. "Harambee"—meaning "pulling together"—is a strong tradition of community self-help in Kenya.

2.   Grandparental care in Britain should not be underestimated. According to a British Broadcasting Corporation (BBC) documentary investigation, on average, school-aged children in Britain spend sixteen hours a week in grandparental care.

Chapter 4

Rethinking the Assignment of Paraprofessionals

Ensuring Students Are Well Served within Budget Constraints

Peter J. Bittel, EdD, Nicholas D. Young, PhD, EdD, and Michael Neiman, PhD

Shrinking resources, both financial and human, have limited educators' abilities to invest in further educational improvements. Several authors have recently underscored that, for further school improvement to occur, administrators need to find more efficient ways of investing increasingly scarce dollars. Given the lack of credible evidence demonstrating the efficacy of many improvement efforts (Robelen, 2002; Schuman, 2004), school leaders remain largely left to their own devices to address the challenge of improving schools with resources that cannot plausibly keep pace.

School leaders must examine all areas of practice to promote greater accountability and efficiencies, especially the ones involving staff that are at times one level removed from direct classroom or special needs instruction and may constitute up to 4% of school operating budgets: paraprofessionals. This is not to suggest that paraprofessionals do not play a vital role in offering needed supports for students, but their utilization must be thoughtful, systematic, and based on student need.

This chapter explores methods to ensure the appropriate assignment of paraprofessionals with particular emphasis on programmatic outcomes and fiscal responsibility.

PARAPROFESSIONAL PROTOCOL FOR PROMOTING PLACEMENT DECISIONS

This protocol is presented as a practical tool to assist school-level administrators in recognizing and developing the skills for the most effective and efficient use of paraprofessional supports within their buildings. The assignment, utilization, and monitoring of paraprofessional supports requires extreme vigilance from all stakeholders. However, it is ultimately the designated responsibility of the principals, assistant principals, and other staff (hereafter, referred to as the administrative designee) to ensure that this very expensive aspect of any district's delivery system is managed appropriately.

An essential element of this protocol is the consensus of terminology between district-wide staff and building-level personnel. The protocol must be viewed as a tool to measure and quantify student needs, not necessarily the staffing needs of a building or department. Aside from the fiscal implications, having students assigned paraprofessional supports has legal implications as well.

This paraprofessional protocol is designed to meet the needs of students with educational disabilities. It was also designed to ensure that students receive an education in the least restrictive environment (LRE) within the context of a free appropriate public education (FAPE).

It is imperative for all school personnel to promote a climate that is practical and not to prescribe services beyond those that are absolutely necessary and appropriate based on the student's needs. Furthermore, from a civil rights perspective, the uniform assignment of paraprofessional protects the district from claims of unfair or inequitable provision of services based on variables external to student need (e.g., a vociferous educational advocate).

The research on inclusion presents the practitioner with many considerations that may seem to warrant adding adults to a student's educational experience. However, a change in pedagogy does not always warrant paraprofessional staffing requirements. The protocol outlined will provide quantifiable accountability if it is used with consistency and a clear understanding of the needs of the student.

PROTOCOL ASSUMPTIONS

Utilization of paraprofessional supports should be fluid, because the assignment of paraprofessionals is inherently determined by student needs, which are, by definition, ever changing:

1. Paraprofessional supports, like all special education services, are meant to be a service, not a place;

2. The programmatic and fiscal aspects associated with the paraprofessional supports must be monitored regularly (every three months or as required) because such oversight benefits both the student and the district;

3. The concepts of efficient and effective paraprofessional utilization are not mutually exclusive;

4. As with any performance accountability measure, decisions regarding the appropriate assignment and utilization of paraprofessionals must be data driven and devoid of subjective variables;

5. A clear understanding of the criteria for the assignment and utilization of paraprofessionals between district personnel and building personnel has to be agreed upon to ensure successful outcomes.

The assignment of paraprofessional support basically falls into two categories: individual-shared assignments related to the assignment of a paraprofessional to a specific student or students; and teacher-classroom assignments referring to the assignments of paraprofessionals to support classroom instruction. The two areas will be addressed as separate entities. However, regardless of whether a paraprofessional is assigned to students or classrooms, the systematic and cyclic heuristic of baseline measurement, follow-up, and reconsideration applies to both types of utilization.

One-on-One and Shared Paraprofessionals: Baseline Measures

The assignment of a one-on-one or shared paraprofessional is made by the individualized education program (IEP) team and must be linked to the following protocol. As stated previously, the fluidity of paraprofessional staffing will generate significant dialogue. If terminology of the protocol is agreed upon, the subjectivity of paraprofessional assignments will diminish. The IEP team must be clear in developing quantifiable student outcomes consistent with the terms outlined in the protocol.

Should the objective data reveal that a one-on-one or shared paraprofessional is warranted, IEP goals and objectives that promote student independence specifically linked to the protocol must be included in the student's IEP. This way, all IEP stakeholders including parents will have quantifiable, operational, and objective goals specifying the appropriate and desirable finite outcome of the assignment of paraprofessional supports. For illustrative purposes, sample independent goals may include

• The student will reduce his/her dependency on a paraprofessional by demonstrating the skills in the area of need with fading prompts from physical to gestural (modeling) as measured by the baseline data and review;

- The student will reduce his/her dependency on a paraprofessional by demonstrating the skills in the area of need with fading prompts from gestural to verbal as measured by baseline data and review;
- The student will reduce his/her dependency on a paraprofessional by demonstrating the skills in the area of need with fading prompts from verbal to independent as measured by baseline data and review;
- The student will increase his/her level of independence from the paraprofessional by reducing the number of prompts needed from three to one as measured by baseline data and review.

Follow-Up Measures

At the end of each marking period, designated staff members, each with sufficient training in the protocol measures and who are familiar with the student's academic, social, and emotional needs, will

1. Assess the student's progress in attaining the stated objectives;
2. Report the student's progress in attaining these goals on the progress notes (which, by law, will need to be sent home along with the student's other progress toward attaining the goals and objectives on the IEP);
3. Report the data to the school administrator.

This will require significant buy-in and training of regular education staff including classroom teachers and specialty area educators. The time frame aligned to the school's marking periods provides for solid summative analytical review of the student's progress.

The concerns are as much a regular education issue as they are a special education issue, particularly where students spend significant time in the regular education setting.

Reconsideration

The designated administrator or other responsible staff member will review the follow-up measures against the baseline performance of the student. Should demonstrable progress be indicated, the administrator will reference the rubric to determine if the assignment of the paraprofessional needs to be adjusted. If an adjustment is required, the IEP team will reconvene and make the determination to reduce, expand, or eliminate the one-on-one or shared paraprofessional supports accordingly.

Communication between building-level administration and district personnel must be fluid and regular. Because staffing decisions have district implications, particularly in the course of a school year, a mechanism for reporting out such data must be developed between the school and the district office responsible for the assignment of paraprofessionals. Systemic collaboration requires structured time to discuss the ever-changing staffing needs and their implication for district programming and budgetary requirements.

The evaluative process should continue until such time that one-on-one or shared paraprofessional supports are not required, or continue if the student's level of need is chronic and indicates that the services are required indefinitely. Essentially, each marking period, administrative and other leadership personnel are reassessing staffing needs related to the growth and progress of the students and related IEP based on the agreed-upon terms outlined in the protocol.

Teacher-Classroom Assignment Measures: Baseline Measures

The schedules, including any revisions, of all paraprofessionals are submitted to the administrative designee to ensure that the resources are being used effectively and efficiently. Each paraprofessional is responsible for regularly providing, via a common reporting procedure developed by the district, data regarding the following parameters:

- The specific classroom(s) that the paraprofessional has been assigned to for each period or block throughout the day;
- The subject that is being taught and daily variations;
- The number of students with IEPs for each period or block;
- The number of weekly minutes of special education instruction each student has with an IEP and the subject addressed via special education services;
- A breakdown of other assignments required of the paraprofessional during the day.

Note: The following figures were developed as a partnership between the Holyoke Public Schools located in Holyoke, Massachusetts, and Futures Education. The authors chose to honor this partnership between the district and Futures by crediting the Holyoke Public Schools in the figures offered as guidelines for monitoring and utilizing paraprofessionals most effectively. Such recognition does not constitute proprietary rights.

Holyoke Public Schools
Professional Support Assessment

Child's Name:

Date of Birth:

SASID #:

Current Placement:
_ Mainstream classroom
_ Self-contained class
_ Resource Room
_ Inclusion classroom
_ Inclusion support
_ Therapeutic Services
_ Health Plan
_ Integrated Preschool
_ Paraprofessional

Directions: Using the student's current educational placement, special education services, and IEP goals, check off the following areas where additional adult support will be needed. Each area checked will need to be an area of concern addressed in the student's IEP.

Additional adult support needed	Social/Emot/Behavior	Communication	Act of Daily Living	Health/Safe/Medical
_ Large group academic support	_ Implementing a highly structured behavior plan	_ Expressive/ Receptive Comm.	_ Feeding	_ Feeding tube
_ Small group academic support	_ Aggressive	_ Augmentative Communication Device/ PECS/ Sign	_ Toilet training	_ Seizure disorder
_ Independent work	_ Destructive behavior		_ Changing (student is incontinent)	_ Flight risk/Puts self in danger
_ Assistive Technology (personal computer & software)	_ Self-Injurious		_ Dressing	_ Health plan
	_ Peer Interactions		_ Mobility (wheelchair bound or braces requiring the use of crutches)	_ Transitions out of classroom
	_ Attention Issues			_ Safety concerns during Specials
	_ Implementing a highly structured sensory diet (per OT)			

Total _____	Total _____	Total _____	Total _____	Total _____
		Grand Total _____		

No assistance needed

Assistance level.   Increased adult assistance
                    Shared assistance
                    Individual assistance
% of the day: _____

Figure 4.1 Paraprofessional Support Assessment

This figure was designed to provide a formalized assessment of the need for paraprofessional support. The rater is responsible for determining the present educational placement and rating the student's needs in five identified domains:

1. Whether additional support is requested for a specific educational activity (large group, small group, independent or assistive technology);
2. Social/emotional/behavior;
3. Communication;
4. Activities of daily living;
5. Health/safety/medical

Each of the five evaluated domains is further broken down by activities, behavior, and performance that may warrant further consideration, with one point assigned to each noted concern. As described below, the type of setting is considered when interpreting the final score.

Holyoke Public Schools – Student Services Division 2004 – 2b
Paraprofessional Assignment Guide for General Education Classrooms

Percentage of Paraprofessional Support		Configuration Options		
Increased Adult Assistance (IAA)		**Increased Adult Assistance (IAA)**	**Shared Assistance**	**Individual Assistance**
Score	Percentage of the day	Support of only 1 student in need of (IAA) can be met using Team Teaching Model (2 teachers in the classroom all day)	Can be shared with 2 other (IAA) students in the same classroom with a total score not exceeding 23 or 100% of the day	Can be met by assigning 1 paraprofessional for 100% of the day
5	15%			
6	20%			
7	25%			
Shared Assistance		Assign no more than 3 students in need of (IAA) per Paraprofessional in the same class or 2 (IAA) students in multiple rooms	Can be shared with 1 other "shared para" students in the same classroom with a total score not exceeding 23 or 100% of the day	Can be shared with 1 student in need of (IAA) & not exceeding a total score of 23 or 100% of the day
Score	Percentage of the day			
8	30%	1 student in need of (IAA) can be assigned with a paraprofessional providing Individual Assistance in the same classroom with a score not exceeding 23 or 100% of the day		
9	35%			
10	40%			
11	45%			
12	50%			
Individual Assistance				
Score	Percentage of the day			
13	55%			
14	60%			
15	65%			
16	70%			
17	75%			
18	80%			

General Education Classroom

Criteria

5-7   Increased Adult Assistance

8-12   Shared Assistance

13+   Individual Assistance or review
of current placement

Figure 4.2 Paraprofessional Assignment Guide for the Regular Education Classroom

This figure provides a guide for interpreting paraprofessional assessment ratings for the general education classroom setting. The final or total score from figure 4.1 should be interpreted with three configuration options:

1. A score of 5-7 suggests increased adult assistance may be needed,
2. A score of 8-12 suggests that shared assistance may be required, and
3. A score of 13 or higher suggests that individual assistance or a review of the current placement option may be appropriate. Furthermore, individual scores also suggest the percentage of the day paraprofessional services may be appropriate. A score of 13, for example, suggests individual assistance may be appropriate for 55% of the school day.

Holyoke Public Schools – Student Services Division 2004 – 2c
Paraprofessional Assignment Guide for Integrated Preschool Classrooms

Percentage of Paraprofessional Support

Increased Adult Assistance (IAA)

Score	Percentage of the day
11	15%
12	20%
13	25%

Shared Assistance

Score	Percentage of the day
14	30%
15	35%
16	40%
17	45%

Individual Assistance

Score	Percentage of the day
18	50%
19	55%
20	60%
21	65%
22	70%
23	75%

Configuration Options

Increased Adult Assistance (IAA)	Shared Assistance	Individual Assistance
Assign no more than 3 students in need of (IAA) Per Paraprofessional in the same class	Can be shared with 2 other (IAA) students in the same classroom not exceeding 100% of the day	Can be met by assigning 1 paraprofessional for 100% of the day
1 student in need of (IAA) can be assigned with a paraprofessional providing Individual Assistance in the same room not exceeding 100% of the day	Can be shared with 1 other "shared para" students in the same classroom not exceeding 100% of the day	Can be shared with 1 student in need of (IAA) & not exceeding 100% of the day

Integrated Preschool Criteria

11-13	Increased Adult Assistance
14-17	Shared Assistance
18+	Individual Assistance

Figure 4.3 Paraprofessional Assignment Guide for the Self-Contained Classroom

This figure provides suggestions for program placement, adult assistance, shared assistance, and individual assistance as well as the percentage of the day that paraprofessional support may be needed for preschool-aged students in a preschool classroom (in reference to Figure 4.1).

Holyoke Public Schools – Student Services Division 2004 – 2c
Paraprofessional Assignment Guide for Self-contained Classrooms

Percentage of Paraprofessional Support

Increased Adult Assistance (IAA)

Score	Percentage of the day
11	15%
12	20%
13	25%

Shared Assistance

Score	Percentage of the day
14	30%
15	35%
16	40%
17	45%

Individual Assistance

Score	Percentage of the day
18	50%
19	55%
20	60%
21	65%
22	70%
23	75%

Configuration Options

Increased Adult Assistance (IAA)	Shared Assistance	Individual Assistance
Assign no more than 3 students in need of (IAA) Per Paraprofessional in the same class	Can be shared with 2 other (IAA) students in the same classroom not exceeding 100% of the day	Can be met by assigning 1 paraprofessional for 100% of the day
1 student in need of (IAA) can be assigned with a paraprofessional providing Individual Assistance in the same room not exceeding 100% of the day	Can be shared with 1 other "shared para" students in the same classroom not exceeding 100% of the day	Can be shared with 1 student in need of (IAA) & not exceeding 100% of the day

Integrated Preschool Criteria

Below-13	Increased staff for Inclusion into Mainstream
14-17	Shared Assistance
18+	Individual Assistance

Figure 4.4 Paraprofessional Guide for the Self-Contained Classroom

This figure provides suggestions for program placement, adult assistance, shared assistance and individual assistance as well as the percentage of the day for students in a self-contained classroom (in reference to Figure 4.1).

CONCLUSION

Paraprofessional services appropriately assigned will enhance student achievement and provide necessary support to the classroom teacher. Depending upon assessment findings, there are times when paraprofessional services are not only needed but in fact essential.

The use of paraprofessionals in regular classrooms can go a long way toward breaking down the walls that often serve to divide special and regular education by demonstrating how such services can have a positive impact on all students, including those with special needs, directly in the classroom setting. At the same time, this chapter underscored that paraprofessional services can be potentially detrimental when provided to students who would be better served through a change of placement or who do not require an enhanced level of support.

The addition of a paraprofessional in a general classroom may also become a barrier to a student's personal independence and social and educational progress while drawing from a finite pool of fiscal resources. As highlighted throughout this chapter, the key is to systemically monitor the initial assignment of paraprofessionals, and then to periodically reexamine the need for their continuation, to ensure the provision of the best possible learning environment and allocation of budgeted funds.

REFERENCES

Bowman, D. H. (2003). "Minnesota Scrambles to Revamp Standards." *Education Week*, 22 (23), 15, 20.

Olson, L. (2003). "All States Get Federal Nod on Key Plans." *Education Week*, 22 (41), 1, 20.

Robelen, Erik W. (2002). "Rules Clarify Changes on Teacher, Paraprofessional Qualifications." *Education Week*, 21 (43), 36.

Shuman, D. (2004). "American schools, American teachers: Issues and perspectives." Boston, MA.

POINTS TO REMEMBER

- *Paraprofessional services may constitute up to 4% of a district's annual operating budget and thus warrant careful monitoring just like other educational programs and investments.*
- *School districts rarely have protocols to determine when paraprofessional services would be beneficial or when such services should be removed to avoid having a negative impact on the academic and social/emotional growth and development of the students receiving such services. Determining and tracking the ongoing need for paraprofessional services in-*

volve a standardized protocol that considers information gathered through a baseline measurement, follow-up, and reconsideration information steps.

- *Ensuring that paraprofessional services are efficient and ensuring that they are effective are not mutually exclusive concepts. Schools can do the right thing for students while being judicious in allocating personnel and fiscal resources.*

Chapter 5

Methods to Meet the Budget Challenges in Special Education

Peter J. Bittel, EdD, and Herbert Levine, PhD

THE FINANCIAL STATUS QUO

The familiar scenario usually plays out like this: each fall the superintendent discusses with the board guidelines and assumptions for the upcoming budget. The board, in collaboration with the superintendent, considers the guidelines and assumptions with the invariable goal of achieving fiscal constraint. Subsequently, when the board reconvenes, it discovers that due to mandates and regulations the special education department's line item is double or triple that of other general education departments submitted.

Then, out of necessity, the board is forced to pillage the general education and maintenance budgets to fund the special education budget. The familiar scenario continues: school board members then go to the community, explaining to the public that special education costs are sacrosanct and that general education costs need to remain flat or be decreased except for what is needed to fund collective bargaining agreements.

Although there can be no doubt that many expenditures devoted to special education are unavoidable and necessary, many of the solutions generally thought to be a special education problem reside in the purview of general education. With the advent of initiatives promoting inclusion and response to intervention (RtI), the alignment of special and general education is a strategic one and, if done right, can be cost-effective.

Moore-Brown states in her research in the *Journal of Special Education Leadership* (2011) that the list of factors contributing to the funding crisis in special education is both familiar and staggering to consider:

1. Funding formulas, which are inequitable, disparate, complex, and inadequate;
2. Legal costs, which are unparalleled in almost any other areas of education;
3. Limitations in funds allocated to hire instructional and administrative staff;
4. Costs for unending training needs, including research-based instructional methods, improved diagnostic procedures, legal requirements, and more;
5. Uncontrolled cost of nonpublic or private placements;
6. Specialized technology and training for students and staff;
7. The need for discretionary dollars to recruit and retain qualified staff;
8. Negotiated salary rises which reflect on budget sheets as increases in the costs of the special education program.

Noted educational finance theorists Odden and Clune (1995) report in their article in *Educational Researcher* that educational financial experts believe that high administrator and teacher salaries are not a primary reason, as some people claim, for the fiscal challenges facing public education.

Instead, they point to the alternative factors: poor resource distribution, unimaginative use of existing funds, school bureaucratic structures, and too great a focus on services with labor-intensive practices that drive up costs. Furthermore, they note that unstable governance structures, lack of incentives to find efficiencies in budgeting, inefficient reporting practices, and tendencies to backload (i.e., purchase materials out of preceding years' budgets) add significant roadblocks to optimizing fiscal responsibility.

GROWING AND COSTLY MANDATES

Special education mandates are not new. However, for budgeting purposes, we must go back to 1975 when PL 94-142 (the Education for All Handicapped Children Act) was enacted. Later, modifications of the original legislation (i.e., Individuals with Disabilities Education Act [IDEA], IDEA Part B, and No Child Left Behind [NCLB]) were passed with many promises and a feel-good ideology.

Despite the federal government's well-intentioned promise to contribute 40% to special education funding under IDEA and NCLB, the reality is that they have only provided approximately 10% of costs for special education.[1] The deficit in anticipated funding has left the remaining burden to be absorbed by state and local entities. Municipalities, many believed to be in a deep recession, are struggling to fund the district portion.

According to a 2004 Center for Special Education Finance report, special education enrollment and expenditures have grown steadily since the implementation of IDEA. Total special education expenditures have been growing far faster than general education expenditures. The primary reason is the increasing enrollments and the identification of special education students. The same report notes:

> The increase in enrollments of special education students, ages three through twenty-one, as a percentage of total student enrollments can be attributed to several factors, including rising numbers of at-risk school-age children, and the birth to three programs served through IDEA Part B. Special education expenditures have demonstrated steady increases paralleling and likely caused by this steady, uninterrupted growth in enrollments. In the 2001–02 school year, the fifty states and the District of Columbia spent approximately $50 billion on special education services alone, and $78.3 billion on all educational services required to educate students with disabilities. (pp. 18–22)

According to the Special Education Expense Project (2003), conducted by the US Department of Education, per pupil special education average costs range from $9,558 to $20,095. Per these calculations, the average special education student cost 1.91 times more to educate than a general education student.

CURRENT PREDICTIONS: A STATISTICAL EXERCISE

According to the National Education Association's website, students enrolled in special education programs have risen 30% over the last ten years. Three out of every four students with disabilities spend part, or all, of their school day in a general education classroom. In turn, nearly every general education classroom across the country includes students with disabilities.

Based on the 2009 National Center for Education Statistics report, 6,483,372 students were supported under IDEA Part B (students from ages three to twenty-one). This represents 13.2% of all students nationwide. From a statistical perspective, the authors used the aforementioned 1.91 factor cited in the US Department of Education report. Although the average cost predicted by the US Census Bureau for a general education student is approximately $12,000, Adam Schaeffer, a policy analyst with the Cato Institute in 2010, believes that average number is deceiving.

Real spending per pupil ranges from a low of $12,000 in Phoenix and some southern cities to over $27,000 in some towns in New York. By using the average of $12,000 per student and multiplying that by the 1.91 factor, this represents a cost of $22,920 per special education student. For statistical purposes, if one takes the 6,483,372 students in special education nationwide and multiplies this by $22,920, we are projected to spend approximately $149 billion in special education funding annually.

Using a more conservative cost factor of 1.50, the national cost for special education programs approximates $117 billion—quite a shortfall as it relates to the contribution of over $11 billion from the federal government. When one considers the original federal pledge to fund 40% of the special education burden, this would have amounted to a federal contribution of $47 billion. The reality of the 10% contribution (i.e., $17 billion) means quite simply that state and local entities need to make up the $30 billion shortfall in the face of a perfect storm of dwindling state and local resources.

IMPLICATIONS FOR SPECIAL EDUCATION COSTS

Superintendents are caught in the funding crossfire, competing for scarce resources. The cost of special education has much to do with the dilemma of how to educate all students with finite resources. Moreover, within the line items of special education expenditures are the following seminal programmatic and logistical realities: (1) low staff-to-student ratio; (2) increased reliance on related services; (3) transportation costs; and (4) outplacement of students. Considered in total, all significantly contribute to the skyrocketing cost of special education services.

In some cases, the addition of paraprofessionals is a self-fulfilling prophecy. Principals want to fix the problem in their building regardless of cost. Their actions often contradict district-wide special education department philosophies and standards for staffing. Building administrators tend to err on the side of their constituents like parents and advocates, which frequently causes conflicts between district policies and the building administrators. The proliferation of paraprofessionals and special education team teaching has placed a real financial burden on local budgets.

Reaching across the IEP Table: Winning Hearts and Minds

Most principals and parents believe that expenditures devoted to special education are inevitable. Attempts to institute cost-cutting measures are emotional exercises fraught with significant resistance from parents and advocates, as well as special and general educators and related service providers.

Many parents come to the individualized education program (IEP) meeting with a sense of entitlement, or perhaps belligerence, toward special education services. Although administrators may perceive that there is overutilization, parents and advocates view any reduction of services or programs suspiciously; in effect, they view these discussions as cynical, cost-driven directives from the superintendent to eliminate their student's services.

The fix must begin with a cultural change stemming from dialogue that is collaborative and transparent. The reality of the situation is special education costs can no longer be ignored and these tough discussions can, and must, occur.

McKenzie and Bishop in *The School Administrator* (2009) state, "If you focused solely on cost containment, parents and teachers might interpret your narrow focus as a lack of commitment to program quality. Often when a superintendent, mentions costs, parents and teachers fear financial concerns will overshadow students' needs. Superintendents need to identify cost-savings opportunities that would not compromise quality" (pp. 16–19).

Because the persons facilitating the IEP process at each school are making the most important resource decisions, superintendents need to exert influence and management oversight to assure that all team leaders (principals, assistant principals, psychologists) are making decisions that are consistent with district standards. As discussed in chapter 1, it is best practice for the superintendent to assure that all team leaders and special education personnel are defining disabilities using codified and district-wide criteria.

Perhaps the most significant prerequisite to enacting uniform criteria is to invest in professional development. Central office special education administrators must play an active role in disseminating the agreed-upon criteria and philosophy to the building staff. In general, the following systemic areas are critical in ensuring that students are afforded every possible opportunity to remain with typical peers while simultaneously assuring free appropriate public education (FAPE) through maximizing finite resources and personnel.

Early Reading Interventions and Expectations

Ensure strong reading and language arts instruction prekindergarten through grade three (and perhaps beyond) to prevent gaps in reading and language achievement. Establish an expectation that students read at grade level by the end of grade three, and continue reading instruction as long as necessary to ensure students meet reading standards.[2]

Implementing Response to Intervention (RtI)

RtI is a general education process that provides educational support and instructional interventions for all students. The RtI framework is robust, and may be adapted to address student needs across a virtual limitless array of skills (e.g., speech improvement, handwriting, reading support, extended school day, summer reading). Tracking the results of the interventions over a defined period of time will help central office and school administrators adjust interventions accordingly.

Monitoring the Appropriateness of Services

In many districts, well-meaning adults are providing services to students who are not entitled to services, providing services that go beyond FAPE, or providing services beyond what is prescribed in the IEP.

While the law specifies mandates surrounding eligibility for services, there are no mandates that specify the extent of the services. No student is entitled to special education or related services if they have not been properly classified as having a disability in accordance with state and federal law. A special education committee charged with formulating an IEP must prescribe the services at a level appropriate to the needs of the student.

Continuous Monitoring

Establish clear performance benchmarks for students and monitor performance with increasing frequency and intensity for students not meeting district standards. With respect to special education, data at both the student (i.e., are the instructional components of IEPs being met) and district (i.e., the adequate yearly progress, or AYP, subgroup) levels must be reviewed just as thoroughly.

Implement Differentiated Instruction

Because students process, acquire, and use information in different ways, classroom instruction must be differentiated to meet the needs of every student. It will require a significant level of professional development for both general and special education staff members.

Hiring

Hire staff that understand and are aligned with the collaborative vision. Ask relative and pertinent questions of new hires to assure congruency, even for contracted employees. Attempt to maintain unity of purpose with scheduled meetings. Itinerant staff can lose significant time in their cars traveling between buildings. This should be examined on an ongoing basis in order to maximize face time with students.

Scheduling of Staff

Allow master schedulers and team chairs to work together to develop cost-effective and instructionally sound scheduling of staff. From both efficiency and programmatic standpoints, a task analysis of staff will help determine if inefficiencies correlate with provision of services that exceed the standards of FAPE.

Consider Implications of In-District and Out-of-District Placements

If a student requires extensive staffing within the district, being placed out of district may bring about an opportunity to reduce staff. Conversely, a student entering the school district from an out-of-district placement or another district could require additional staff or the redeployment of existing staff. In fact, some districts have been entrepreneurial by bringing students in from other districts to defray costs of their in-district programs. In all cases, it is important to keep track of projected student placements and caseloads through monthly tracking devices.

Transportation

Special education transportation is both a huge undertaking and one with a significant upside to identifying savings. At a minimum, it is critical that special education transportation providers collaborate with the district's transportation coordinator to create efficiencies in the cost of transporting special needs students. This topic is discussed at length in chapter 8.

Align Strategic Goals between General and Special Education

Special education programs and services can be improved using the same processes that are used in general education programs. A superintendent can gather special education data from a programmatic level and then direct the improvement of programs to short- and long-term strategic improvement plans. Information related to program effectiveness needs to be reviewed and analyzed regularly. Adjustments to curriculum, instructional strategies, teacher training, and professional practice can yield significant improvements in student performance.

Budgeting: Understand the Nuances of Special Education Programs

Include the special education administrators and other special education leadership personnel in the budget development cycle and process by having them project and quantify programs, services, and placements by student. Identify the students individually who will require more services or fewer services, or those students who may require the same level of service. When reviewing the special education budget consider the following:

- Does the staffing pattern maximize efficiency?
- What are the patterns for substitute services for both certified and non-certified staff?
- Is the district collecting any medical insurance or Medicaid for those services eligible?

- Are legal services being preapproved by the superintendent or designee, or do administrators rely too heavily on cursory calls to the district lawyer?
- Are too many students being tested?
- Does the professional development budget align with district initiatives and are there ways to defray the cost of professional development by using collaboratives or sharing the costs with neighboring districts?
- Are itinerant staff spending a good part of their day traveling between buildings?
- How efficient is the transportation system?
- Can some out-of-district placements be returned to creative in-district programs?
- Are supplies and equipment being purchased through a collective bidding process?
- Is there an overwhelming duplication of dues and fees?
- Can district memberships be substituted for individual memberships to professional organizations?

NEXT STEPS

Despite the successful implementation of the aforementioned processes, it is likely that the costs of special education will continue to outpace the costs of general education. In such a scenario, the superintendent may be forced to seek additional out-of-the-box options.

Private-Public Partnership

One creative avenue was pursued by McKenzie and Bishop (2009), who operate an educational service center in Massachusetts. The writers note, "Private-public partnerships for special education and related services provided a solution. Although the organization experienced difficulties during the decision-making process the benefits of private-public partnership have outweighed any problems" (pp. 16–19).

Some districts have outsourced paraprofessionals, speech and language therapists, occupational therapists, physical therapists, nurses, and audiologists. Districts that have implemented private-public partnerships of personnel find that the resultant management, accountability, and efficiency of the purchased services outweigh any negatives.

Shared Services through a Collaborative

According to McKenzie and Bishop (2009), "The collaborative's primary purpose is to expand the quality of education in its member districts. To that end, we provide special education programs and career and technical education programs for students on the premise that numerous educational services can be offered more effectively and efficiently by pooling resources" (pp. 16–19).

Superintendents' networks and regional special education consortia can offer districts the opportunity to house programs or send students to a collaborative run by the district or the regional service center, or through a private-public partnership.

All the programs need to be carefully monitored by district staff to ensure that students' IEPs are being met and that students are transitioned back to their home school when appropriate. Ultimately, the goal is to promote student access to the least restrictive environment—which is generally recognized as the student's neighborhood school.

Develop External-Independent Partnerships

There are a host of private consulting services that offer school districts in-depth examinations of costs and programs, and may consequently provide opportunities for cost avoidance. The methodologies may vary, but typically include qualitative interviews of stakeholders and quantitative reviews of financial records.

Due diligence necessitates that district leadership ensures the prospective consultants possess a record of accomplishment of successes in other districts that include past reports detailing clear findings and practical recommendations. Some partners offer school districts the educational, clinical, management, and cost-containment expertise necessary to meet the needs of growing numbers of special needs students within the confines of limited state, federal, and local funding.

All activities should be conducted with the goal of providing services that are effective in the most efficient manner within the context of the district's vision and direction.

The perceptions that special education costs are out of control and inevitable must be addressed deliberately. In addition to the procedural (e.g., RtI) and programmatic (e.g., identifying partnerships) steps a district can enact to mitigate spiraling costs, it is important that communication is optimized in diffusing the erroneous concept that special education is insulated from reasonable cost scrutiny. Communication with all stakeholders regarding the fiscal, legal, and programmatic realities of special education enhances transparency and support.

Specific topics that may be presented at board meetings or other forums to enhance transparency and understanding include

- What are the categories of disabilities in the district?
- Why must the district supply adaptive technology?

- Why are students placed out of district?
- Why does the district have to transport special education students to out-of-district placements?
- What is inclusion?
- Does the state provide any funding to the district?
- Why does the district have to provide homebound instruction?
- What is the role of team chairs?
- What is building-level decision-making?
- How does the district's special education expenditures compare to other like districts?
- What are related services?

REFERENCES

Center for Special Education Finance Report (2004). http://csef.air.org.

Chambers, J., Y. Kidron, and A. Spain (2004). "Characteristics of High-Expenditure Students with Disabilities, 1999–2000." *Special Education Expenditure Project: Report 8*. Submitted to Office of Special Education Programs, US Department of Education.

McKenzie, A., and A. Bishop. (2009). "Outsourcing School Services." *The School Administrator*, 66, no. 9: 16–19.

Moore-Brown, B. (2011). "Case in Point: The Administrative Predicament of Special Education Funding." *Journal of Special Education Leadership*, 14, no.1.

Muller, E. (2007, August). "Reading First and Special Education: Examples of State-Level Collaboration." InForum, US Department of Education.

National Instructional Materials Accessibility Standard Report (2004, October 14). Version 1. US Department of Education.

Odden, A., and W. Clune (1995). "Improving Educational Productivity and School Finance." *Educational Researcher*, 24, no. 9: 6–10, 22.

Schaeffer, Adam B. "They Spend WHAT? The Real Cost of Public Schools." The Cato Institute. March 10, 2010. http://www.cato.org/publications/policy-analysis/they-spend-what-real-cost-public-schools.

Total Expenditures for Students with Disabilities, 1999–2000: Spending Variation by Disability Special Education Expenditure Project (SEEP), Report 5 (2003, June). Prepared for the United States Department of Education, Office of Special Education Programs. http://csef.air.org/publications/seep/national/final_seep_report_5.pdf

POINTS TO REMEMBER

- *Create a culture that is transparent and is inclusive, including staff from both general education and special education. The budget and finances have an impact on the entire district.*
- *Develop a dialogue and be part of the financial conversation. The superintendent's voice and vision must lead the dialogue.*
- *Develop job-embedded special education professional development that deals with finance, staffing, and scheduling to create efficiencies across all programs.*

- *Develop external partners. Too often internal staff are too acculturated and committed to their own mission. Private companies and service centers can provide the external partner needed.*
- *Use data as a tool to inform and decide. A regular flow of data from the special education department to the superintendent must be systemic and regularly updated.*

NOTES

1. The US Department of Education in the 2011–2012 budget allocated $11.7 billion for special education aid to states.

2. The research shows that strong primary reading programs lower the special education propensity levels. See Muller (2007).

Chapter 6

NCLB and IDEA

Related Services and the Law

Peter J. Bittel, EdD, Erin Edwards, MA, CCC/SLP, Michael Neiman, PhD, Herbert Levine, PhD, and Wendy C. Reed, Esq

Superintendents and educational leaders across the country by now are familiar with a major tenet of the No Child Left Behind (NCLB) Act, which asserts that all students, including children, adolescents, and young adults with disabilities, are considered to be general education students first.

Special education and related services are to be provided to students with disabilities solely so that they can benefit from the special education curriculum (Mele-McCarthy, 2007a). In addition, NCLB holds schools, school districts, and states accountable for the academic achievement of all students. "Therefore, all students, including those with disabilities, must be included in the State accountability system; all students count and must be counted" (Mele-McCarthy, 2007a, p. 4).

We often speak globally about related services and clinicians. Specifically, related service providers (RSPs)—a cadre that includes speech and language pathologists and assistants, occupational therapists and assistants, and physical therapists and assistants—by definition play a pivotal role in the provision of supports and interventions designed to enhance a student's ability to access the general education curriculum and demonstrate academic achievement.

The roles of the clinicians are integrally tied to ensuring the development of an individualized education program (IEP), to ensuring that services are delivered in the least restrictive environment, and to ensuring appropriate

Chapter 6

accommodations are provided during instruction and assessment (American Physical Therapy Association, 2009; American Speech-Language-Hearing Association, 2007; "Occupational Therapy in School Settings," 2010).

DEFINING "THE WORK"

In the wake of the reauthorization of the Individuals with Disabilities Education Act (IDEA) in 2004, clinicians were faced with the need to focus increasingly on the issues involved in providing services via an educational model as opposed to a medical or clinical model (Means, 2006). Key provisions of the reauthorization further required RSPs to focus on eligibility issues, to participate in manifestation hearings, to participate in prereferral processes, and to provide increased accountability for student outcomes (Klotz and Nealis, 2005).

The implications of both NCLB and IDEA on the practice patterns of clinicians and on the overall delivery of related services are complicated, and in many ways are a work in progress. This chapter will present the implications through a consideration of the historical and legal contexts surrounding NCLB and IDEA, through a sketch of the roles and responsibilities of RSPs within special education programming, and through a discussion of the major components of school-based practice that have been affected by this legislation.

Such discussion surely may support a contention that is crucial for educational leaders to understand today: that "becoming proficient in understanding the requirement of NCLB [and IDEA], being involved in conversations about solutions to the conundrums, and incorporating the precepts of the law into our practice will go a long way toward advancing our students" (Moore-Brown, 2004, p. 10).

The Education of Children with Disabilities—A Broad Perspective

In 1970, there were approximately eight million children with disabilities in the United States, four million who were not receiving an appropriate education, and another one million who were excluded from public education altogether (Essex, 2008; Imber and Van Geel, 2010). Many of the children who did receive some form of public education were unable to realize its full benefit, either because their disabilities had not been accurately diagnosed, or because appropriate supports were not in place to meet their needs (Essex, 2008; Smith, 2005).

Prior to landmark legislative and legal efforts that began in earnest during the 1970s, the educational needs of millions of children were not being met. Schools continued routinely to exclude children with disabilities from the educational setting, allowing only children with mild impairments to participate in regular classrooms. Children with moderate disabilities received little more than custodial care in school, and children with significant needs were referred to institutions (Valentino, 2006).

During this time, special education was a mere footnote in US educational statistics. There were fewer than 3.5 million children with disabilities served in public schools, mostly in isolated, self-contained settings, and teacher preparation for special education was a minor activity (Smith, 2005).

In the early 1970s, the exclusion of children with disabilities from public education became the target of a number of lawsuits, most notably *Pennsylvania Association for Retarded Children (PARC) v. Commonwealth of Pennsylvania* and *Mills v. Board of Education.* As Imber and Van Geel (2010) have summarized, the cases did differ somewhat, but the major findings by the courts in both instances were similar:

- Students were excluded from public schools because they had disabilities;
- The effect of such policy was wholly to deprive these students of access to a publicly funded education;
- The government's purpose in excluding them was to save money;
- Excluding children with disabilities from school was not rationally related to the goal of saving money because uneducated people were likely to become a much greater financial burden on the state than if they had been educated; and therefore
- Exclusion of children with disabilities from public schools violated the Equal Protection Clause.

The legal opinions ultimately included the outline of both substantive and procedural requirements designed to ensure that children with disabilities would be admitted to public schools and provided with appropriate educational services tailored to their individual needs. Schools subsequently were required to follow specific procedures when classifying students with a disability, deciding on appropriate placements, and reclassifying and/or changing placement (Hall, 2007).

The *Mills* and *PARC* cases were part of a larger nationwide effort that included both lawsuits and political efforts to secure more appropriate educational services for children with disabilities. This effort has resulted in four major federal statutes designed to ensure effective education and equal access for children with disabilities (Hall, 2007; Imber and Van Geel, 2010; Valentino, 2006) with IDEA having the greatest potential impact on the provision of related services to children who qualify for special education:

1. The Rehabilitation Act of 1973 (specifically Section 504, commonly referred to as simply 504). Section 504 defined the necessity to provide supports for students who do not qualify for an IEP, but who still require some modifications and accommodations to fully participate in the classroom;

2. The Americans with Disabilities Act of 1990 (ADA) is a federal law that in part requires states to provide special education consistent with federal standards as a condition of receiving federal funds;

3. The Individuals with Disabilities Education Act (IDEA) was originally passed in 1975 and has been extensively updated and amended since. The original title of this act was the Education for All Handicapped Children Act (EAHCA), and has also been known as the Education of the Handicapped Act (EHA). In 2004, the name was officially changed to the Individuals with Disabilities Education Improvement Act (IDEIA);

4. The No Child Left Behind Act of 2001 (NCLB) first emerged conceptually as the Elementary and Secondary Education Act (ESEA) in 1965, and has been reauthorized approximately every five years since then.

Specific Supports for Children with Disabilities — The Implications

Since the signing of the No Child Left Behind Act of 2001, increasing national attention has been focused on education. The legislation is based upon the belief that all students can learn—and the definition of *all students* includes students who come from lower socioeconomic backgrounds, students who do not speak English as a first language, and students with disabilities (Mele-McCarthy, 2007a).

With the provisions inherent in both IDEA 1997 and IDEIA 2004, educators must ensure that all children, including those with significant cognitive disabilities, have the opportunity to participate and progress in the general curriculum (Clayton et al., 2006). Congress passed IDEA in an effort to clearly define the responsibilities of school districts regarding children with disabilities, and to provide a measure of financial support to assist states and localities in meeting these obligations (Valentino, 2006).

As a side note, however, it is interesting to consider that NCLB's promise in relation to funding was woefully inadequate. While many communities, especially minority communities, continue to play catch-up by running hard just to stay in place, the same communities are being left behind due to severe resource constraints. Little effort is evident in the funding streams to help states provide incentive plans for high-quality teachers—the requirement of which is a cornerstone of both NCLB and IDEA (Gray, 2005).

Further, NCLB originally promised that schools labeled "in need of improvement," and thereby subject to "corrective action" for their failure to make adequate yearly progress (AYP), would receive funds to put programs in place to address these shortcomings. However, although "NCLB authorized $500 million per year in school improvement funds for this purpose, for the first five years of NCLB, the total amount actually appropriated to school improvement funds is exactly zero. Nada. Zilch" (Packer, 2007, p. 3).

The Purpose of IDEA and What It Means for School Districts

Relative to the specific supports for children with disabilities, IDEA might be viewed as consisting of five major tenets:

- First, the measure is intended to ensure that all children with disabilities have available a free appropriate public education (FAPE) designed to recognize and meet their unique needs, and prepare them for post-secondary experience (Gartin and Murdick, 2005; Huefner, 2008; Mele-McCarthy, 2007a);
- Second, the measure is intended to ensure that the rights of children with disabilities and their parents are protected (Imber and Van Geel, 2010; Turnbull III, 2005);
- Third, the measure is intended to assist states in the implementation of a statewide, comprehensive, multidisciplinary, and interagency system of early intervention for infants and toddlers with disabilities and their families (Mandlawitz, 2007);
- Fourth, the measure is intended to ensure that educators and parents have access to the necessary tools to improve education results (Mele-McCarthy, 2007a; Zirkel, 2007b);
- Fifth, the measure is intended to ensure that methodologies and strategies are in place to assess and ensure the effectiveness of efforts to educate children with disabilities (Daniel, 2008; Gray, 2005).

In summary, IDEA is entitlement legislation that supports students with disabilities, beginning with the identification of educational need, to the delineation of specialized instruction and supports via the individualized education program to provide FAPE to the student, and to assist in the transition to post-secondary activity.

The Purpose of NCLB and How It Affects Related Services

NCLB, on the other hand, has a different stated purpose. This legislation was designed to ensure that all children have a fair, equal, and significant opportunity to obtain a high-quality education and to reach, at minimum, proficiency on challenging state academic achievement standards and state academic assessments (Imber and Van Geel, 2010; Moore-Brown, 2004).

NCLB further states that this overarching purpose can be accomplished by "ensuring that high-quality academic assessments, accountability systems, teacher preparation and training, curriculum, and instructional materials are aligned with challenging state academic standards so that students, teachers, parents, and administrators can measure progress against common expectations for student academic achievement" (Mele-McCarthy, 2007a, p. 2).

NCLB further mandates that states demonstrate AYP toward a national goal that in 2014, all students will be at least proficient in reading/language arts and math by meeting the educational needs of all students including the ones in high-poverty districts, students with limited English proficiency, migratory students, students with disabilities, and neglected or delinquent students (Donlevy, 2002; Essex, 2008; Hess and Finn, 2004).

> The statute explicitly mandates that states establish performance goals for children with disabilities consistent with the goals and standards set for all children. Specifically, the state must establish goals for the performance of children with disabilities that are the same as the state's definition of adequate yearly progress. This must include the state's objective of progress for children with disabilities consistent, to the extent appropriate, with any other goals and standards for children established by the state. (Daniel, 2008, p. 2)

There is a potential conflict between IDEA and NCLB as it applies to students with disabilities. On the one hand, IDEA requires schools to provide individualized educational programming depending on the unique needs of the student, and on the other hand, NCLB requires that there be statewide standards of proficiency in reading and math—in effect, uniform learning goals for all students, including students with disabilities (Imber and Van Geel, 2010; Means, 2006).

Philosophically, IDEA was designed to assess individual progress, to provide for appropriate remediation, and to document measurable progress. NCLB, however, was designed to implement specific state standards, to assess school district progress as a whole, and to remediate to reach grade-level proficiency (Means, 2006). Regardless, NCLB considers students with disabilities to be a designated subgroup whose performance must be assessed as part of the process to determine whether a particular school is making AYP (Mandlawitz, 2007).

It perhaps is more helpful to view NCLB and IDEA at their confluence, which from the perspective of special education programming might be viewed in the context of their synergistic relationship.

"In effect, it can be said that IDEA 2004 holds the general education teacher and the general education curriculum responsible for teaching reading/language arts and math to all children, under the auspices of NCLB, while IDEA protects the individual rights of children with disabilities through identification and provision of special education and supplemental supports and services to enable a child with a disability to be involved in and progress in the general education curriculum" (Mele-McCarthy, 2007a, p. 3).

THE ROLE OF RELATED SERVICE PROVIDERS

It is clear that NCLB and IDEA have resulted in a number of challenges for all special educators, including related service providers. Both pieces of legislation are predicated on improving the educational success of both regular and special education students, and even though they have fundamentally different purposes, both laws emphasize accountability, measurable outcomes, and meeting specific standards, all of which apply specifically to both the direct and indirect services provided by related service professional staff.

The promise that every student will learn and succeed has been translated into public policy via NCLB and IDEA. Therefore, at least in theory, students with disabilities are assured of access to the curriculum upon which specific standards are based, access to the assessments that measure performance on those standards, and inclusion in the reported results that determine how well a school or school district is meeting the established performance criteria (Rosenberg, Sindelar, and Hardman, 2004).

Further, NCLB holds individual schools, school districts, and states accountable for improvements in student achievement, with a particular emphasis on closing the achievement gap between high- and low-performing students, and children from disadvantaged groups, including those with disabilities (Simpson, Lacava, and Graner, 2004).

Unfortunately for related service providers, however, the specific details of implementation of these laws are necessarily unclear since neither law specifically outlines the role of the related service provider (Means, 2006). To provide further context for the impact of IDEA and NCLB on the delivery of related services in public schools, it is helpful to consider the specific roles and responsibilities of related service providers within special education programming.

There is broad agreement within the three certifying organizations for the major related services—the American Physical Therapy Association (APTA); the American Occupational Therapy Association (AOTA); the

American Speech-Language-Hearing Association (ASHA)—regarding the fundamental roles and responsibilities of these professionals (APTA, 2009; ASHA, 2007; "Occupational Therapy in School Settings," 2010):

   Critical Roles: *RSPs have integral roles in education and are essential members of school faculties.*

- **Working across all levels**—RSPs provide appropriate intervention services in prekindergarten, elementary, middle, junior high, and high schools with no school level underserved. (Note: in some states infants and toddlers would be included in school services.)
- **Serving a range of disorders**—As delineated in the scopes of practice for each particular discipline, and as described in most state and federal guidelines, RSPs work with students exhibiting the full range of communication, fine motor and sensory, and gross motor disorders; myriad etiologies may be involved.
- **Ensuring educational relevance**—The litmus test for roles assumed by RSPs, per the dictates of IDEA and NCLB, is whether the disorder has an impact on the education of students. Therefore, RSPs address the academic, developmental, and functional needs of students that have a potential impact on attainment of educational goals.
- **Providing unique contributions to the curriculum**—RSPs provide a distinct set of roles based on their focused expertise in language, sensory integration, and mobility.

Range of Responsibilities: *RSPs help students meet the performance standards of a particular school district and state.*

- **Prevention**—RSPs are integrally involved in the efforts of schools to prevent academic failure in whatever form those initiatives may take, for example, in response to intervention (RtI) initiatives. RSPs use evidence-based practice and peer review strategies in prevention approaches.
- **Assessment**—RSPs conduct assessments in collaboration with others that help to identify students with particular disorders as well as to inform instruction and intervention, consistent with evidence-based practice.
- **Intervention**—RSPs provide intervention that is appropriate to the age and learning needs of each individual student and is selected through an evidence-based decision-making process. Although service delivery models are typically more diverse in the school setting than in other settings, the therapy techniques are clinical in nature when dealing with students with disabilities.

- **Program design**—It is essential that RSPs configure school-wide programs that employ a continuum of service delivery models in the least restrictive environment for students with disabilities, and that they provide services to other students as appropriate.
- **Data collection and analysis**—RSPs, like all educators, are accountable for student outcomes. Therefore, data-based decision making, including gathering and interpreting data with individual students, and overall program evaluation are essential responsibilities.
- **Compliance**—RSPs are responsible for meeting federal and state mandates as well as local policies in performance of their duties. Activities may include IEP development, Medicaid billing, report writing, and treatment plan/therapy log development.

The Legal Context for Related Services Supports

Given this understanding of the specific roles and responsibilities of RSPs, and to further appreciate the impact of NCLB and IDEA on the practice of physical, occupational, and speech therapies, it is also important to recognize the legal context in which the disciplines practice within public schools.

First, consider how the "meaningful benefit standard" applies to related service practice within public schools. As detailed by Daniel (2008), in *Polk v. Central Susquehanna Intermediate Unit 1636*, the court ruled in favor of a standard that requires more than a *de minimis* benefit to special needs students—the anticipated benefit of intervention must be meaningful, and therefore, more than trivial progress must occur.

At the same time, however, courts have contradicted the "meaningful benefit standard," stating that IDEA "does not require providing every available service necessary to maximize a disabled child's potential but that a school district cannot discharge its duty by providing a program that provides only *de minimis* or minimal academic achievement" (Daniel, 2008, p. 6).

Second, it is equally important to understand the legal precedence of the seminal *educational benefit* standard applied to the provision of related services in a special education setting. As stated by the Colorado Association of School Boards Legal Services Program (CASB; 2009), "the Supreme Court held that the IDEA is designed to provide disabled children with a 'basic floor of opportunity' that is reasonably calculated to provide a disabled student with some educational benefit, *i.e.*, allow the student to make meaningful and adequate gains in the classroom" (p. D-G-3).

This "floor of opportunity" then is designed to "afford *some* educational benefit, but the outcome need not maximize the child's education . . . and the court also stated that a student is only entitled to *some* educational benefit; the benefit need not be maximized to be adequate" (Daniel, 2008, p. 6).

The most recent case law (*Thompson RJ-2 School District v. Luke P.*; *School Board of Lee County v. MM, 46*) supports the same interpretation of educational benefit. In this case, the courts ruled "that a school district is providing a student with appropriate special education programming if the program is reasonably calculated to allow the student to make 'some progress' on his or her IEP. Thus, the IEP need not provide the student with the best possible educational program, but rather need only provide the student with an educational experience that is appropriate and that allows the student to make some progress" (CASB, 2009, p. D-G-3).

Thus, IDEA does not require school districts to maximize a student's educational potential. It is within this legal context as well as within the context of the scopes of responsibilities presented by the certifying organizations of related service providers that the impact of IDEA and NCLB on the delivery of related services will be discussed.

INFLUENCES OF NCLB AND IDEA ON THE PROVISION OF RELATED SERVICES

The impact on the provision of related services—physical and occupational therapy, and speech and language pathology—of IDEA 2004 and NCLB to children within special education programming can be divided into the following categories:

- **Service Delivery**, including not only the setting in which services are provided, but also the increased focus on academics and the utilization of assistive technology;
- **IEP Process**, including content, as well as philosophical and pedagogical components;
- **Accommodation and Assessment Processes**, including eligibility for alternative procedures as well as the foundation of accountability;
- **Quality of Teaching**, which speaks to the qualifications of related service providers and what the new legislation says, and does not say, regarding RSP professionals (Klotz and Nealis, 2005; Means, 2006).

Service Delivery

Since students with disabilities must be held to state and district standards, it stands to reason the RSPs should develop goals and objectives to ensure students meet the standards. While the foundation of the assessment standards rests on curriculum information—which, according to IDEA, should be the cornerstone of intervention—it does not imply that RSP intervention should teach the assessment to the student, but that intervention should be designed to allow the students to learn the curriculum and to understand the testing formats (Means, 2006).

The overarching goal of both special education teachers and RSPs, through the IEP process, should be to help students understand the nature of their disability and how it affects learning and access to grade-level content. "The goals in the student's standards-based IEP reflect the strategic instruction the student requires to attain grade-level content information and skills and to interact effectively with others. When students with learning disabilities are taught learning strategies in a systematic, intensive fashion, they demonstrate gains in academic achievement, including performing at or near grade level in literacy areas" (Hall, 2007).

IDEA clearly states that goals and objectives must be aligned with the general education curriculum, a requirement presenting challenges for clinicians who were trained in a medical or clinical model of service provision as opposed to an educational model. Only the educational model focuses on functional skill development and enhanced access to the curriculum (Brigham et al., 2004; David, 2005; Means, 2006; "Occupational Therapy in School Settings," 2010).

While there is a danger that RSPs may be pressured to focus more on academics as opposed to therapeutic intervention to compensate for time out of class (Brigham et al., 2004; Courtade and Ludlow, 2007), the increased emphasis on an educational model of service provision is often translated into a more collaborative and integrated approach to addressing goals and objectives.

Plug-in, push-in, and/or co-teaching models or, more correctly stated, an *inclusive model* avoids the disruption to students who would otherwise miss critical instruction in the classroom, as related services are provided within the general education classroom (David, 2005; Hall, 2007). These models effectively blend the general educator's expertise in pedagogy and content areas with the RSP's expertise in strategic instruction and strategies to adapt both instruction and instructional materials to increase access to grade-level content for all students.

While less integrated in approach, the *pull-out model*—in which students are removed from the general education setting, for the purposes of providing therapeutic intervention, whether in a small group or one-on-one setting—is still appropriate if the model is clinically defensible in light of IDEA's requirements (Gartin and Murdick, 2005; Mandlawitz, 2007; Zirkel, 2007a). The learning strategies identified in the IEP provide the focus in this model, which also involves (1) direct services to students including instruction, intervention, and evaluation; (2) indirect services to students to support the implementation of the IEP; and (3) indirect activities that support students in the least restrictive environment and the general education curriculum (Means, 2006).

The IEP Process

The individualized education program (IEP) serves as the blueprint for providing a free appropriate public education to individuals with disabilities, and is the child-specific foundation of a student's special education program (Gartin and Murdick, 2005; Zirkel, 2005).

Despite the fact that the original IDEA legislation required the individualization of programming for special needs students via the IEP, challenges remain for special educators in achieving the goal of individualization. "Indeed, our own experience with several school districts that pride themselves on the quality of their IEPs suggests that the 'I' in IEP could more accurately stand for 'interchangeable.' Perhaps the interchangeability of IEPs is a necessary reflection of the movement to include students in the general education curriculum; perhaps it is the result of limited time, imagination, or training" (Brigham et al., 2004, p. 6).

Given the challenges inherent in the dictates of IDEA as they relate to the specificity of programming for individual students and the effects of such dictates on RSP service provision, it is important to understand IDEA's impact on the components of the IEP and the IEP process, and the subsequent impact on the responsibilities of the related service providers:

- **An increased focus on function and positive outcomes**. The updated IDEA requires RSPs to increase emphasis on the need for general and special education programs to have challenging expectations that lead to productive and independent adult lives.

  The concepts of *academic achievement, functional performance*, and *developmental needs* now take precedence over simple "educational performance" (David, 2005). Emphasizing that both academic and functional performance levels be included clarifies the vague *educational performance* term used in the 1997 amendments.

- **Goals and short-term objectives/benchmarks**. Prior to the most recent iteration of IDEA, all IEPs were required to include specific, measurable annual goals and accompanying short-term objectives or benchmarks for each area of need as described in the present level of performance section of the IEP.

  The major change in the updated version of IDEA is the removal of the requirement that all IEPs include short-term objectives or benchmarks for each annual goal (Earles-Vollrath, 2004; Klotz and Nealis, 2005; Smith,

2005), unless the child will be participating in an alternative form of assessment in lieu of the mandated district and state tests (Hyatt, 2007). Annual goals have been clarified to be academic and functional goals that are designed to enable the child's involvement and progress in the general education curriculum, and meet each of the child's other educational needs that result from the child's disability (Gartin and Murdick, 2005).

- **Evidence-based practice**. RSPs are required by IDEA 2004 to assure that special education and related services are based upon peer-reviewed re-search when available. The stipulation is in accord with the NCLB focus on the need for empirically validated intervention techniques (Huefner, 2008), and further suggests that school officials in general will not be able to justify services based upon what they deem to be acceptable.

  Requiring schools to base services upon peer-reviewed research requires educators to do more than just open the door to public education for students with disabilities. Instead, IDEA requires authorities to research and consider best practices, not simply those that are adequate or will only produce some progress (Valentino, 2006).

- **Accommodations on assessments**. As experts in the assessment of both skill and deficit areas for children with disabilities, RSPs work with both special and general education teachers designing accommodations for stu-dents with disabilities to participate effectively in state- and district-man-dated assessment activities (APTA, 2009; ASHA, 2007; "Occupational Therapy in School Settings," 2010).

  Without associated accommodations, children would more likely be as-sessed on their disability instead of on their knowledge of the requisite educational content. The IEP must include a statement of any individually appropriate accommodations necessary to measure the academic achieve-ment and functional performance of the child on state- and district-wide assessments (Gartin and Murdick, 2005).

- **Dates, times, and duration of services**. Although no specific changes were made to the most recent iteration of IDEA relative to the requirement that the IEP include the projected date for the beginning of the specified services (both special and related), it does now require RSPs to provide a description of the frequency, location, and *duration* of the services and modifications (Gartin and Murdick, 2005).

- **Transition services**. IDEA requires that transition services be addressed in the IEP in the year in which the student turns sixteen (David, 2005). RSPs must address clinical concerns relative to a coordinated set of activities for students with disabilities focused on successful transition from high school to post-secondary opportunities.

- **IEP meeting attendance**. In the past all IEP team members were required to attend each and every IEP meeting. With new provisions in IDEA 2004, if the parent and the local educational agency (LEA) agree, the attendance of a team member whose input is not considered essential is no longer mandatory.

  Further, a specific member of the team may be excused from attending the IEP meeting even if his/her specialty is being considered if the parents and LEA agree, and the team member provides a written report to the parents and IEP team prior to the meeting (Gartin and Murdick, 2005; Hyatt, 2007).

The Accommodation and Assessment Processes

Both NCLB and IDEA 2004 require accommodations for students with disabilities. Accommodations are specialized procedures in presentation, response, setting, and timing or scheduling assisting equitable access for students with disabilities during both instruction and assessments. The accommodations are intended to reduce or eliminate the effects of a student's disability, not to reduce learning expectations (Hall, 2007).

The role of the IEP team including the RSPs is to determine *how* the students will participate, not *if* they will do so (Mele-McCarthy, 2007b). The law limits the numbers who qualify for alternative assessments to ensure the allotment is reserved for the benefit of students most in need of adaptations (Clayton et al., 2006; Means, 2006).

As summarized by Hall (2007), IEP teams are supported in the accommodation and assessment process via guidelines provided by the Office of Special Education Programs of the US Department of Education. The responsibilities of the IEP team and specifically the RSPs are reflected in the following basic steps:

- Expect that students with disabilities will achieve grade-level academic standards, and develop/select accommodations in the assessment process that will reflect this expectation;
- Learn about accommodations for instruction and assessment, how such accommodations support specific learning needs, and the potential impact on state and local assessment scores;

- Select accommodations for instruction and assessment for individual students, remembering that only the accommodations that reduce the effect of the student's disability may be selected;
- Administer accommodations during instruction and assessment, focusing on the logistics of accommodations use before, during, and after the assessment to ensure that accommodations are applied in a standardized manner;
- Evaluate and improve accommodations used to determine and ensure that the accommodations are in fact effective and appropriate and result in the student's increased access to the general education curriculum.

Quality of Teaching

IDEA requires that all students with disabilities receive a free and appropriate education, individualized to their specific needs, and delivered in the least restrictive environment. "At the heart of the issue is the belief that an education cannot be appropriate, least restrictive, or procedurally compliant without qualified teachers and other qualified personnel to provide it" (Jameson and Heufner, 2006).

NCLB mandated that all students in the nation's schools must be taught by highly qualified teachers who have content knowledge in the academic subjects for which they are responsible, in addition to state teaching certification at the grade levels to which they are assigned (Courtade and Ludlow, 2007; Hyatt, 2007). Although NCLB is silent with regard to specific qualifications of special education teachers, IDEA stipulates that the highly qualified standard applies to every teacher, including special education teachers (Rosenberg, Sindelar, and Hardman, 2004; Valentino, 2006).

Both NCLB and IDEA are equally silent regarding the highly qualified provision as it applies to related service providers, but clearly the provision is an attempt to ensure the hiring and retention of effective teachers who are highly qualified in their field or discipline, and who can demonstrate competency. It would seem then that both NCLB and IDEA would default to individual states and the guidelines surrounding qualifications for licensure of related service providers (Means, 2006).

Both speech and language pathology and occupational therapy are currently master's level professions, although a number of clinicians at the bachelor's level remain who are "grandfathered in" and who can legally practice in a variety of clinical settings without graduate education (ASHA, 2007; "Occupational Therapy in School Settings," 2010). The discipline of physical therapy has recently become a graduate-level profession, although as with the disciplines of speech and language pathology and occupational therapy, many physical therapists currently practice with only a bachelor's degree as a result of the grandfathering process (APTA, 2009).

A bachelor's level education in any of the disciplines does not appear to meet the spirit or intent of the highly qualified provision of IDEA, but the definition of the provision clearly defaults to individual state licensure and certification laws (Means, 2006).

CONCLUSION

Accepting the premise that the provisions in both NCLB and IDEA serve to promulgate higher standards for the education of students with disabilities, related service providers play a pivotal role in designing and providing the supports necessary for students with disabilities to demonstrate achievement within the context of these higher standards.

REFERENCES

American Physical Therapy Association. (2009). *Guidelines: Physical Therapy Scope of Practice* (Scope of Practice). Retrieved from APTA: www.apta.org.

American Speech and Hearing Association. (2007). *Scope of Practice in Speech Language Pathology* (Scope of Practice). Retrieved from ASHA: www.asha.org.

Brigham, F. J., W. E. Gustashaw III, A. L. Wiley, & P. Brigham. (2004). "Research in the wake of the No Child Left Behind Act." *Behavioral Disorders*, 29(3), 300.

Clayton, J., M. Burdge, A. Denham, H. L. Kleinert, & J. Kearns. (2006, May/June 2006). "A four-step process for accessing the general curriculum for students with significant cognitive disabilities." *Teaching Exceptional Children*, 38(5), 20.

Colorado Association of School Boards Legal Services Program (2009). "Practical Guidelines and Analysis: Free Appropriate Public Education." www.casb.org.

Courtade, G. R., & B. L. Ludlow. (2007). "Ethical issues and severe disabilities: Programming for students and preparation for teachers." *Rural Special Education Quarterly*, 27(1/2), 36.

Daniel, P. T. (2008). "'Some Benefit' or 'Maximum Benefit': Does the No Child Left Behind Act render greater educational entitlement to students with disabilities." *Journal of Law and Education*, 37(3), 347.

David, K. (2005). *IDEA 2004, P.L. 108-446: Impact on Physical Therapy Related Services* (Fact Sheet Summary). Retrieved from APTA: www.apta.org.

Donlevy, J. (2002). "Teachers, technology and training: No Child Left Behind: In search of equity for all children." *International Journal of Instructional Media*, 29(3), 257.

Earles-Vollrath, T. L. (2004). "IDEA 1997 and related services." *Intervention in School and Clinic*, 39(4), 236.

Essex, N. L. (2008). *School Law and the Public Schools: A Practical Guide for Educational Leaders* (4th ed.). Boston, MA: Pearson Education, Inc.

Gartin, B. C., & N. L. Murdick. (2005). "IDEA 2004: The IEP." *Remedial and Special Education*, 26(6), 327.

Gray, L. H. (2005). "No Child Left Behind: Opportunities and threats." *The Journal of Negro Education*, 74(2), 95.

Hall, S. (2007). "NCLB and IDEA: Optimizing success for students with disabilities." *Perspectives on Language and Literacy*, 33(1), 35.

Hess, F. M., & C. E. Finn. (2004). "Inflating the life rafts of NCLB: Making public school choice and supplemental services work for students in troubled schools." *Phi Delta Kappan*, 86(1), 34.

Huefner, D. S. (2008). "Updating the FAPE standard under IDEA." *Journal of Law and Education*, 37(3), 367.

Hyatt, K. J. (2007). "The new IDEA: Changes, concerns, and questions." *Intervention in School and Clinic*, 42(3), 131.

Imber, M., & T. Van Geel. (2010). Education Law (4th ed.). New York: Routledge.

Jameson, J. M., & D. S. Heufner. (2006). "'Highly qualified' special educators and the provision of a free appropriate public education to students with disabilities." *Journal of Law and Education*, 35(1), 29.

Klotz, M. B., & L. Nealis. (2005). "The New IDEA: A summary of significant reforms." *National Association of School Psychologists*.

Mandlawitz, M. (2007). *What Every Teacher Should Know about IDEA 2004 Laws and Regulations*. Boston, MA: Pearson Education, Inc.

Means, J. (2006). "The impact of IDEA 04 and NCLB on speech and language related services: How do we meet the challenges." *Forum on Public Policy: A journal of the Oxford Round Table*.

Mele-McCarthy, J. A. (2007a). "Approaches to assessment: IDEA and NCLB." *Perspectives on Language and Literacy*, 33(1), 25.

Mele-McCarthy, J. A. (2007b). "NCLB assessment of accountability: Good teaching or teaching to the test?" *Perspectives on Language and Literacy*, 33(1), 11.

Moore-Brown, B. (2004). "Becoming proficient in the lessons of No Child Left Behind." *Perspectives on School-Based Issues*, 5(1), 7-10.

"Occupational Therapy in school settings." (2010). Retrieved from www.aota.org.

Packer, J. (2007). "The NEA supports substantial overhaul, not repeal, of NCLB." *Phi Delta Kappan*, 89(4), 265.

Rosenberg, M. S., P. T. Sindelar, & M. L. Hardman. (2004). "Preparing highly qualified teachers for students with emotional or behavioral disorders: The impact of NCLB and IDEA." *Behavioral Disorders*, 29(3), 266+.

Simpson, R. L., P. G. Lacava, & P. S. Graner. (2004). "The No Child Left Behind Act: Challenges and implications for educators." *Intervention in School and Clinic*, 40(2), 67.

Smith, T. E. (2005). "IDEA 2004: Another round in the reauthorization process." *Remedial and Special Education*, 26(6), 314.

Turnbull III, H. R. (2005). "Individuals with disabilities education act reauthorization: Accountability and personal responsibility." *Remedial and Special Education*, 26(6), 320.

Valentino, A. (2006). "The individuals with disabilities education improvement act: Changing what constitutes an 'appropriate' education." *Journal of Law and Health*, 20(1), 139.

Zirkel, P. A. (2005, November/December). "What does the law say?" *Teaching Exceptional Children*, 38(2), 60.

Zirkel, P. A. (2007a). "The new IDEA." *Learning Disability Quarterly*, 30(1), 5.

Zirkel, P. A. (2007b, January/February). "What does the law say?" *Teaching Exceptional Children*, 39(3), 61.

POINTS TO REMEMBER

- *With the reauthorization of IDEA, clinicians' roles have changed. They are now charged with the requirement to practice within an educational model as opposed to a clinical or educational model—goals and objectives must be tied to the student's need to access his or her curriculum.*

- *The definitions of free appropriate public education (FAPE) and least restrictive environment (LRE) must be considered in the context of placement discussions for students who qualify for special education, as well as in clinical decisions surrounding the frequency and duration of related services.*

- *NCLB and IDEA are similar in that both pieces of legislation are predicated on improving the educational success of both general and special education students. Both laws emphasize accountability, measurable outcomes, and meeting specific standards, all of which apply specifically to both the direct and indirect services provided by related service professional staff.*
- *The updated IDEA requires related service providers to recognize an increased emphasis on the need for general and special education to have challenging expectations that lead to productive and independent adult lives. The concepts of academic achievement, functional performance, and developmental needs now take precedence over simple educational performance.*
- *The "A" in a FAPE has legal precedent defined as adequate, reasonable, and required for a student to access his or her curriculum. Districts are not compelled to attempt to maximize the educational benefit of services for a student beyond that definition.*
- *Appropriate supervision, management, and oversight are key components of successful related services delivery systems and should include outcome data from each clinical provider.*

Chapter 7

Superintendents' Use of Special Education Data and Performance Measures in an Environment of Accountability

George David Jack, MEd, MBA

Data and performance outcomes are the measures of accountability for the many constituencies that superintendents serve. According to Englert and colleagues (2003), the purpose of data is to assist the superintendent in determining the policies and practices that districts use to meet new accountability demands. The degree to which superintendents use policies and practices should be research based and validated as effective and purposeful.

The current milieu of discussion surrounding accountability and performance measures has particular application in the special education arena. Although staff may be inundated with data, most data remains unused, and therefore rarely alters pedagogical behavior. The purpose of this chapter is to outline a data protocol that will maximize superintendents' oversight capacity regarding special education by creating data systems that are understandable yet meaningful.

THE ATTRIBUTES OF GOOD DATA

Goodwin, Englert, and Cicchinelli (2003) stated there are twelve essential components of good data and performance measure accountability systems. These include the following:

- Clear standards and expectations;

- High-quality assessments aligned with standards;
- Multiple measures;
- High expectations for *all* students;
- Data that is readily understandable to the public;
- Diagnostic utility yielded by the data;
- Sanctions and awards linked to results;
- Flexibility that allows for differences and creativity;
- Alignment of resources, support, and assistance for improvement;
- Balance in design of data;
- Support from stakeholders;
- Uniformly applied collection, analysis, and application processes.

Goodwin, Englert, and Cicchinelli (2003) elaborated upon six constructs of good data that have systemic impact and, in the authors' words, "have the most impact on the superintendent." These constructs are discussed below with a particular emphasis on their application to special education.

Systemic Attributes

A superintendent must ensure that valid, clear, and deliberate student data-gathering processes are in place in order for the data to provide the most utility. Systemic processes provide the critical foundation to ensure that data is appropriately gathered, and assure valid and real-time oversight of all pedagogical endeavors, including the ones relating to special education.

High-Quality Assessments

Central to an assessment of performance is a system that explicitly aligns student outcomes with curricular expectations. Because most special education students spend the majority of their days in the general education environment, differentiated instruction coupled with high-quality assessments must be the norm. According to most researchers, teacher-prepared exams do not measure what the standards, both local and state, require. In addition, teacher-prepared exams frequently do not measure the curricular expectations of a district.

The superintendent must assure that assignments and formative assessments align to curricular standards, which also align to state and federal standards. Because special education students are often given the same assessments as their regular education peers, the effectiveness of differentiated instruction will be validated by analyses of the results.

Multiple Measures

By law, and best practice, multiple measures should be used in the identification of students for special education services. A well-developed, systemic, holistic approach identifying and assessing the obstacles that prevent student learning must be in place.

Academic tests alone should not be the measure used to determine a student's special education identification. Baker and colleagues (2002) stated, "Decisions about individual students should not be made on the basis of one test." Districts must develop a set of assessment protocols that allow all students to demonstrate achievement.

Data That Examines District and School Indicators

School departments are not dynasties, and must be part of a district-wide curricular effort operationalized by relevant indicators. General and special education staff, with principal oversight, should have knowledge regarding the expected outcomes and standards of the district, and provide instruction designed to meet the needs of all students. The superintendent must communicate to the special education director that commonality among schools is paramount. Assessment of student outcomes is a measurement of district standards that is neither site- nor teacher-specific.

Data That Is Understandable to the Public

Educators have their own language and abbreviations. The common terminology and acronyms recognized by special educators (e.g., IEP, FAPE, and LRE) are often a foreign language to the public. Data and corresponding terms presented to the public, particularly parents, must be understandable and personalized to the specific learning needs of each student.

Alignment of Resources

Financial, human, and capital resources should align with the needs of the students, not the needs of the adult community. A monitoring system tracking identification of special education students is critical, given the programmatic and fiscal implications that an over- or under-identification procedure will have on the district. When the appropriation of resources is not systematic, then subjective variables such as parent advocacy will drive decisions at the IEP meeting. A process must be in place across the district that examines resource disparities and disproportionate identification structures.

METHODS TO ACT UPON DATA FOR MEANINGFUL CHANGE

Whether or not a superintendent chooses to use a prepackaged program or develops a data platform internally, management of data must be fluid and user-friendly for all stakeholders. Data has to be concise; too much data obscures meaningful results.

Successful superintendents develop a culture fostering open communication among the superintendent and the central office special education director and staff as well as open sharing of data. In a climate of exploding special education costs, the superintendent is then equipped with data to examine the reasons for any expenditure, determine solutions to provide cost-effective alternatives, and provide the results to the public.

Many superintendents neglect or ignore special education programs and the data generated by the programs. The mantra of "it's mandated" or "I have no control over that program" leads to a rift between general educators and special educators, and diminishes the use of available data to effect change. The superintendent, in unison with the special education administration, must create a system to extract data that is important to the community.

It is recommended that the superintendent and the special education director meet on a regular basis. Scheduled meetings will allow the superintendent time to digest and act upon the data. A superintendent should request and consider data that may be divided according to resources and programs.

Resource Allocation and Staff Management

Because staffing patterns with benefits account for approximately 80% the special education budget, it is incumbent upon the superintendent to examine the ratio of staff to students and conduct building-by-building comparisons. The superintendent may find a tendency for some schools to over- or under-identify special education students.

The special education director should provide building master schedules that include open periods for professional staff members. Although work flows are fluid, it should be discernible whether or not there are staff members who have more than one prep period or who are scheduled for testing with too few cases to assess. Inefficiencies in staff travel should also be determined from schedules. When examining absenteeism, it is possible to identify patterns such as absences on Mondays, Fridays, and before major holidays.

One of the hidden, yet most expensive, mandatory services is special education transportation. As detailed in the next chapter, a thorough analysis of special education transportation may yield significant savings.

An analysis of contracted services may reveal significant cost savings with respect to providers' schedules, staffing patterns, and contractual terms. Also, special education supplies are often purchased separately from the conventional district procurement methodology. Special education supplies should be purchased in accordance with established district purchasing procedures to ensure proper oversight and accountability.

Although district counsel typically provides a valuable and needed service, administrators may become too dependent on very costly legal opinions. Administrators should receive preapproval by the superintendent or a designee to contact the district's legal counsel. In some situations, the state can provide the same information or the special education administrative network can assist. Group purchasing of membership in professional associations might be instituted as only one type of cost-effective measure.

In many instances, Medicaid or other third-party insurance may be accessed to defray the costs of services. Although special education administrators must be accountable for accessing any source of reimbursement available, the superintendent should provide the oversight of such potential revenue streams.

Professional development must be budgeted, utilized, and aligned with school improvement plans. Too often professional development is the first line item frozen during the budget cycle. Professional development needs to be increased during periods of significant reorganization and change within the organization.

PROGRAMS MONITORING AND DATA COLLECTION

Student-specific entry and exit information may be the most critical of all the data a superintendent receives to assist the management of overall special education services. The data should include the following:

1. The number of students by building who have been deemed eligible for services;
2. The number of students that have been, or are projected to be, tested for initial eligibility;
3. The number of students discharged from special education services per month.

These data will provide a better understanding of the numbers of students referred and identified while indicating how the district's prereferral program is operating.

Out-of-district placements individually can cost up to six figures and, with associated transportation costs, place significant strain on the district's total operating budget. Given the fiscal and political concerns surrounding out-of-district placements, data corresponding to rationale for placement, number of students placed, lengths of stay, services, and outcomes must be constantly reviewed to ensure that the placements provide optimal outcomes. Given the financial implications, the number of students receiving home-bound instruction also requires consistent close scrutiny.

In September, districts tend to begin with relatively small preschool class-rooms, but the numbers burgeon throughout the year as students turn three and become the responsibility of the district. The cost of early intervention is often exorbitant. Data received in September should include projections of population increases. In addition, the special education director should ex-plore other cost-effective options such as setting up walk-in services for students who do not require full-day programs.

If a student's skills will regress during summer vacation, the student is eligible for extended school year (ESY) services. Given the associated costs, it is critical that the admission and eligibility data reflect the application of criteria that are established and understood by all stakeholders.

CONCLUSION

The same methodology that determines the most effective way to collect, analyze, and act upon data in a district should, and must, be applied to special education services, resources, and programs. Scrutiny of special education services and costs is critical to ensure a climate of accountability and transpa-rency to the public, and ultimately to provide sound stewardship of finite district funds—funds that are increasingly being earmarked to educate stu-dents with educational disabilities.

REFERENCES

Baker, E. L., R. L. Linn, J. L. Herman, and D. Karretz. (2002). *Standards for Educational Accountability*. Los Angeles: National Center for Research on Evaluation, Standards and Student Testing (CRESST), 3.

Englert, K., D. Fries, B. Goodwin, and M. Martin-Glenn. (2003). *Understanding How Superin-tendents Use Data in a New Environment of Accountability*. Institute of Education Sciences. U.S. Department of Education. Washington, DC.

Goodwin, B., K. Englert, and L. F. Cicchinelli (2003). *Comprehensive Accountability Systems: A Framework for Evaluation*. REL Deliverable #2002-07. Aurora, CO: Mid-Continent Re-search for Education and Learning.

POINTS TO REMEMBER

- *Sort through the mountains of data to get to the data that will help you to make informed decisions about programs and individual students.*
- *Understand the data, and make use of the appropriate data to support student learning.*
- *Know the master schedules, staffing plans, and transportation needs in each building.*
- *Spend the appropriate time with the special education director and building administrators to ensure your understanding of all programs.*

Chapter 8

Special Education Transportation

*Why It Is Expensive and What Can Be Done
to Reduce the Cost*

Richard Labrie, MEd

CURRENT LAWS AND REGULATIONS GOVERNING SPECIAL EDUCATION TRANSPORTATION

The transportation needs of every special education student must be considered as part of the individualized education program (IEP) development process. If the student cannot ride regular buses for medical, safety, or educational reasons, then the IEP team specifies the need for specialized transportation and indicates that the student requires particular transportation related to his or her disability. In some cases the student's behavior intervention plan requires an aide or monitor to accompany the student in the classroom, and this requirement extends to school transportation.

Several laws govern special education transportation. The Individuals with Disabilities Education Act (IDEA) designates transportation as a related service for students with disabilities. The regulations specified in 34 C.F.R. Sec. 300.24 (b) (15) specify that transportation includes

- Travel to and from and between schools;
- Travel in and around school buildings;
- Specialized equipment, such as special or adapted buses, wheelchair lifts, and ramps, if required to provide special transportation for a student with a disability.

Section 504

Section 504 of the Rehabilitation Act of 1973 also addresses transportation services to the extent that these services provide access to education. This law ensures that recipients of federal financial aid do not discriminate against qualified persons on the basis of their disabilities. One of the relevant provisions states:

> No qualified student shall, on the basis of their handicap, be excluded from participation in, be denied the benefits of, or otherwise be subjected to discrimination under any transportation, or other extracurricular or other postsecondary education program or activity.

ADA

The Americans with Disabilities Act (ADA) further clarifies transportation for students with disabilities. ADA prohibits discrimination against all persons with disabilities and applies to all public agencies, including schools. In general, ADA states architectural barriers in and around buildings cannot prevent persons with disabilities from environmental access.

Related Transportation Mandates

Other precedents that support, explain, or clarify school special education transportation services include

- Rulings from the US Department of Education's Office of Special Education Programs (OSEP);
- Rulings from the state department of elementary and secondary education;
- Rulings from the US Department of Education's Office for Civil Rights (OCR);
- State due process hearings, findings, and opinions;
- Federal court decisions;
- State court decisions;
- State laws and regulations governing student transportation.

SCHOOL TRANSPORTATION ENTITLEMENTS

Free Appropriate Public Education (FAPE)

If a school district provides transportation to its general education students, then it must provide transportation for its special education students to any program to which it assigns the students. Even if transportation is not provided to all general education students, a district must decide, on an individual basis, whether or not a special education student requires transportation as a related service in order to receive a free appropriate public education (FAPE).

In short, if a student with a disability requires transportation as a related service, the school district must provide it. In all cases, the school district's obligation under IDEA is not dependent upon whether non-disabled students receive the same type of service. Rather, the obligation is based on the individual needs of the disabled student.

Least Restrictive Setting

When making transportation decisions, school districts should ensure that they have considered the least restrictive setting for the special education program. Under IDEA, each public school has to ensure that students with disabilities are educated with non-disabled students to the maximum extent possible. Removal of students with disabilities from the general education population occurs only when the nature and the severity of the disability is such that education in a general education class cannot be satisfactorily achieved with the use of supplementary aides and services.

Special education programs and services, including transportation, generally require collaboration and consensus among parents, the student (depending on age), educators, and transportation personnel. Most transportation issues are identified and resolved through the IEP process. The IEP should carefully delineate that transportation be required for a student as a related service, but should not go beyond what is medically or educationally required to provide safe and efficient transportation.

For example, parents often want to minimize the time their child spends on a school bus or transportation vehicle, and will frequently request that the student be the last one picked up and the first one dropped off on any route. Such accommodation is only required when a student's disability makes it inappropriate for that student to ride on the vehicle for a longer time than students without disabilities.

If approved by the IEP team, the request can inhibit the district from providing cost-effective routing and scheduling with multiple students on vehicles. The end result is the transportation for one student becomes very costly. As an alternative, if a student with a disability is capable of using regular transportation, IDEA does not require transportation to be listed as a related service in the IEP.

Transportation Costs

Numerous studies have demonstrated that the cost of special education trans-portation greatly exceeds that of regular transportation. The differential ranges from four times to ten times the cost of regular transportation. In fiscal year (FY) 2010, the Washington, DC, school district spent $93,286,476 pro-viding transportation services to 3,682 special needs students requiring out-of-district placements for an average of $25,335 per student. The average transportation cost per regular education student is approximately $200 to $400, depending on the size and demographics of the district. Corresponding special education transportation costs often range from $4,000 to $6,000 per student, again depending on school schedules and district geography and distance to placements.

TRANSPORTATION COMPONENTS

Vehicles and Equipment

The type and size of transportation vehicles are decisions generally left to the school district's discretion. Although there may be specific restrictions in different states, vehicles can include vans, minibuses, private cars, and taxi-cabs. None of the options listed are prohibited by IDEA and, in fact, have been approved in some instances. Districts should consider the impact on least restrictive environment in their choice of vehicles.

When feasible, the district should offer the same modes of transportation to both special needs students and general education students for student integration with the understanding that special equipment may be needed for students with disabilities. Choices include a wide variety of items such as special or adaptive buses, wheelchair lifts, ramps, special types of seat re-straints, security devices such as harnesses, tethers, braces, brackets, seat belts, vests, curb cuts, car seats, locks, handrails, walkers, wheelchairs, air-conditioning, and other climate-control methods including tinted windows.

Personnel to Assist Students

Personnel for specialized transportation may include bus aides, escorts, or bus monitors. If personalized services are needed in a classroom, similar services may be needed in a student's bus for transportation purposes. Such determinations must be made on an individualized basis by the team during the IEP process. The goal of transportation as a related service is primarily to provide safe access to education.

Transportation In and Around School Buildings

The IEP team should consider what type of assistance is required for the student within the school building. The building may need lifts, ramps, curb cuts, elevators, stair tracks, or personal assistance for the student to navigate crowded hallways. School districts are not generally required to provide a wheelchair for transportation purposes outside of school, but may be required to provide one while a student is receiving special education services within the school.

Bus Stop or Door to Door

Transportation encompasses not only the picking up and dropping off of a student before and after school, but also includes components and elements of the IEP. Each school district must determine if a student needs transportation to and from school, and determine what type of vehicle and services are needed in order to facilitate a safe trip. The law is ambiguous regarding whether the district's responsibility ends at the bus stop, at the curb of the student's home, or at the home. Districts should weigh a number of factors in determining the scope of transportation requirements on an individual student basis. However, the safety and welfare of the student must be the most important factor.

Critical questions that IEP teams should consider in reference to student safety are

- Is the student mobile or non-ambulatory?
- What are the effects of the student's age and disability on his or her ability to deal with safety hazards?
- What is the distance traveled, and is it dangerous or difficult terrain?
- Is private assistance readily available?
- Is public assistance available including crossing guards?
- What are the student's general supervisory needs?

FACTORS TO CONSIDER FOR SPECIAL NEEDS STUDENTS RIDING REGULAR BUSES

Unless separation from general education students is necessary due to a student's disability, Section 504 and Title II of ADA generally prohibit separate transportation services for students with disabilities. Among the factors to consider for special transportation are

- Safety of the student;
- Inconvenience and safety of other students riding the bus;

- Needs of the student with the disability including whether mainstreaming opportunities are available;
- Financial burden on the school district;
- Medical issues such as the need for oxygen or other breathing apparatus;
- The need for air-conditioning;
- The length of the ride;
- The need for restraining devices or specialized seating;
- The need for a medical attendee, such as a nurse.

In some cases, such as those where special education vehicles are utilized to provide services for medically fragile students, the IEP may require that appropriate personnel including a student's bus driver receive training such as CPR, seizure control, treatment of allergic reactions, EpiPen administration, and first-aid for medical emergencies.

Exactly what constitutes an excessive daily commute varies greatly due to factors like the nature of the disability, overall health condition, and norms for that region. Nevertheless, a review of published opinions reveals that, with the assumption that the district is not located in a sparsely populated rural area, a student's daily commute generally should not exceed one hour either way.

Augmenting or Shortening the School Day

Shortening the school day to accommodate bus schedules constitutes a denial of FAPE. Students with disabilities must be afforded a comparable length of school day and week to that of their non-disabled peers unless there are compelling and specific reasons that require a modification to the length of the day.

EFFICIENT SCHOOL TRANSPORTATION SYSTEMS

Regardless of a district's size, there are a number of performance measures that are common to student transportation systems. Proper scrutiny and assessment of the variables lead to more efficient transportation and ensure accountability from the operator of the transportation system. Such variables include

Safety:

- Accidents or incidents per 100,000 miles of bus travel;
- Student referrals per 100,000 students bused;
- Annual hours of training for each vehicle driver;
- Number of student discipline referrals.

Cost and Service Effectiveness:

- Operational cost per mile per rider for provider for regular transportation;
- Operational cost per mile per rider for special needs transportation;
- Route riders per mile, regular transportation;
- Route riders per mile, special needs transportation;
- On-time performance;
- Maximum rider trip time;
- Complaints per vehicle.

Maintenance Performance:

- Miles between road calls or breakdown;
- Percent preventative maintenance completed on time;
- Turnover time per bus repair;
- Annual, semiannual, or quarterly Registry of Motor Vehicles inspection reports as each state requires.

CONSORTIUMS

Multidistrict Bidding

A typical bid specification necessitates that the bidder-contractor agrees to work with the school district relative to multidistrict routing, scheduling, and the cost sharing of buses/vans where possible. The practice of route distribution may facilitate shared costs among the participating school districts in order to minimize each school district's costs. Typically, the district reserves the right to place its students on routes and vehicles from neighboring school districts and to accept students from neighboring school districts onto its routes.

Multidistrict Routing and Scheduling

Sharing transportation services among neighboring schools may provide opportunities for cost-effectiveness. Chief among them are reducing special education transportation costs, improving service delivery, increasing management expertise, and acquiring and operating a computerized software system, which may not be affordable for a single district. One of the transportation areas easily divided among districts is a shared service delivery system. In this model, a single group of buses and drivers are used to service multiple school districts for home-to-school and other types of trips. The model has particular utility for out-of-district special education transportation where neighboring districts share common placements.

SHARED RESPONSIBILITY

Another model is shared management services, including the shared costs of a computerized routing and scheduling system and trained personnel. The paradigm makes the delivery system more efficient, and can also be used in conjunction with a shared services model. Shared support services may be expanded to include procurement of buses, billing, payroll, and other types of business-related services. In addition, infrastructure may be shared. For example, there may be a regional bus depot from which the buses from all districts operate, and which includes mechanical fleet maintenance and fueling.

Another common approach is a service consortium—or collaboration—wherein all participating districts agree to establish a stand-alone entity with responsibility for transportation that includes acquisition of buses, insurance, drivers, benefits, and so on. The benefit of the approach is that it is cost-effective and removes any management control bias because no single district is fully responsible for providing all the services. The major drawback of the approach is that it is the most complex of the models to implement given implications for liability, funding, and reporting of a third-party entity.

A third-party contract for service delivery is also an option. The contract can be with a private sector company or a public partnership such as an educational collaborative or a regional service provider. Each state has different organizational structures for regional services. The regional approach provides many of the same benefits of a consortium, but minimizes the complexities associated with establishing a consortium as a separate financial and business entity.

District responsibility can also be simplified through the use of a management-only contract. By hiring a third party to manage the transportation program but leaving ownership of the personnel and the assets with the individual school districts, the management contract may minimize the concerns over loss of control by individual districts. The approach requires a strong partnership agreement that ensures no one district can disproportionately have an impact on other districts if it chooses to withdraw from the agreement. The approach also requires a great deal of trust between the cooperating school districts.

A clear and flexible cost-sharing agreement promotes the fair and equitable allocation of management and operational costs. The premise behind multidistrict routing and scheduling is to reduce the high cost of out-of-district transportation for special education students, improve the quality of transportation services, minimize route overlap congestion, and avoid long and unnecessary delays at pick-up and drop-off sites.

THE CHALLENGES OF MULTIDISTRICT AGREEMENTS

Efforts to achieve greater efficiency by transporting multiple students in the same vehicle across several school districts present numerous challenges. Challenges include students with behavioral issues, significant age differences of students, specific medical conditions, dissatisfaction of districts with the current service providers and prices, and potential concerns of parents. In addition, some districts may possess their own vehicles and drivers, and may be reluctant to share with other districts.

Although multidistrict routing and scheduling has proved to be effective in several states, as a general rule district participation is voluntary. However, the Rhode Island General Assembly recently initiated the creation of a statewide transportation system for out-of-district special education and non-public school students. The legislative amendment is entitled "Transportation of School Pupils beyond City and Town Limits." The requirement for participation by all Rhode Island school districts is mandated by the state.

Several geographic and demographic attributes unique to Rhode Island make this model a viable option given the state's limited total land area, the second-highest state population density in the United States, the highest percentage of special education students by enrollment in the country (21%), and a large non-public-school student population. Motivating the reforms are a desire for improved services to students, more efficient use of state funds, and consolidation of services that are difficult for individual districts to provide in isolation.

The state legislature envisions that eventually all busing for public, non-public, and special education students (for both in-district and out-of-district students) will be operating under the direction of the Rhode Island Department of Elementary and Secondary Education in cooperation with the participating school districts. The plan includes a combination of regional and statewide systems with oversight by one or more systems managers.

Such coordination is representative of increasing statewide partnerships between the Rhode Island Department of Elementary and Secondary Education and the Rhode Island school districts. The program is administered by the Office of Statewide Efficiencies in the Rhode Island Department of Elementary and Secondary Education. Because many of the districts are currently under contract, each district will transition to the statewide program upon termination of current agreements.

The results from the first three years of implementation show a significant decrease in the number of vehicles, resulting in a corresponding reduction in costs to participating districts. A pilot program has been expanded to include regional bidding and service delivery for regular transportation. Initial results indicate a reduction in both the number of buses and the costs. The primary advantage of a multidistrict bidding process is that it creates an economy of

scale leading to increased competition for the contracts. The result has generally been a reduction of costs, or at least cost containment, and more favor-
able terms for contractual negotiations and management.

COMPUTERIZED ROUTING AND SCHEDULING

The routing and scheduling process includes identification of bus stops, assignment of students to bus stops, design of the various bus runs, and the
creation of runs into bus routes. Cost-effective and efficient routing and
scheduling are the primary factors associated with parental and school district satisfaction. However, because the typical transportation contract paradigm is based upon the cost per day per vehicle utilized there is little, if any,
incentive for contractors to maintain a high level of efficiency.

Therefore, the checks and balances process actualized by computer-generated methodology is critical. In national studies, computer-generated routes
have proved to be significantly (32%) more efficient and cost-effective than
hand-developed routes.

N=231 Districts	Utilize Routing Software?	Average Number of Buses per 100 Students
YES	141 districts	1.82
NO	90 Districts	2.4
	Variance	0.58
	Variance %	31.87%

Figure 8.1 Comparison Computer Generated vs. Manual Routing Methods

*Source: Student Transportation Benchmarking Survey, Pennsylvania Asso-
ciation of School Business Officials, Management Partners Services, May
2008

Some districts, depending on demographics, are simply too small to take
advantage of computer routing software. District personnel that do not use
routing software spend an inordinate amount of time manually developing
and managing routes and schedules.

Because route efficiency ultimately determines the number of routes,
buses, and drivers required, it is critical to the overall improvement of transportation cost-effectiveness. In the current economic climate it is important
to maximize the dollars going into the classroom and to minimize the dollars

used for transportation, without compromising quality or safety. In order to increase reimbursements, a district must reduce its route mileage and/or increase the number of eligible riders. Given declining enrollments in many districts, increasing route efficiency might be the only option.

In the absence of a computerized routing system, staff must rely on computer spreadsheets to maintain student and route data. This data is often difficult to maintain and manipulate because student needs and routes continually change. As a general rule, because routing software can significantly reduce the number of man-hours, the transportation supervisor becomes more efficient in managing the day-to-day transportation operation. In short, computer routing systems can help districts

- Develop and manage bus routes, student data, and drivers;
- Visualize bus stops, routes, and students;
- Generate state reports;[1]
- Manage redistricting issues;
- Design routes with an integrated mapping system in collaboration with area school districts for common out-of-district placements.

Once installed and with personnel properly trained, computer routing systems are relatively inexpensive to maintain. In fact, most pay for themselves through savings and future cost avoidance. When comparing system costs, many districts report an immediate savings in consideration of the cost of the man-hours necessary to operate the previous manual routing system.

Application of computer routing will also provide the opportunity to develop "what if" scenarios, such as changes in bell schedules that would provide a larger window of transportation times between tiers. The change, in turn, may allow the district to reduce the overall number of buses in simultaneous operation and consequently reduce the overall cost of transportation. Frequently, a change of only ten to fifteen minutes of a single bell schedule can result in the elimination of several buses.

TRANSPORTATION AUDITS

Despite the application of internal checks and balances, it may be advisable for a school district to commission an audit by a third party in order to determine whether it is operating an efficient and cost-effective transportation system.

Among district practices leading to transportation inefficiencies are

- Lack of computerized routing and scheduling software;
- Reliance on the contractor to design routes and schedule students;

- Lack of training of the person in charge of route design and scheduling;
- Inefficient or unnecessary bus stops;
- Accommodation of parental requests that are not medically or educationally necessary.

The following recommendations are commonly offered in order to maximize the efficiencies of a school transportation system:

- Establish an adequate bus replacement plan;
- Manage the transportation department staffing;
- Establish efficient bus routes and schedules utilizing computer routing systems;
- Utilize multidistrict routing and scheduling and cost sharing whenever possible;
- Implement regular driver and mechanic training programs;
- Establish and implement a vehicle maintenance plan;
- Measure and monitor a transportation department's performance;
- Adhere to state reporting requirements;
- Evaluate the plausibility of privatization of transportation as opposed to self-operated systems.

A typical transportation audit or efficiency study employs a methodology that includes both a quantitative review of various documents and reports as well as a qualitative assessment based on discussions with administrators and the current contractors.

The scope of work for a transportation audit may include

- A review and analysis of the current transportation costs and related contracts;
- A review of any current transportation or related issues or problems;
- A review of the current transportation routes, driver qualifications, compensation, vehicle specifications, and efficiencies;
- A cost comparison of current contracts to recent private contractor bids for similar transportation services with area school districts;
- A review of the last transportation bid and quotation process or bid process for special education transportation;
- Recommendations for improved efficiencies and/or cost reductions.

Irrespective of the scope of the study, the following measures can be used in such an analysis:

- Assessment of the district's transportation policies with reference to state minimum standards;

- Adequacy of reported operational information to secure state transportation aid;
- Cost-effectiveness of pupil transportation services by type of transportation: regular and/or special needs, including cost per mile, cost per bus, and cost per student;
- Bus capacity and utilization;
- Comparative bus driver wages and benefits;
- Effectiveness of coordination between the special education and transportation departments to ensure efficient transportation of special needs students;
- Effectiveness and efficiency of transportation routing;
- Manual or computerized routing;
- Use of municipal transportation services;
- Assessment of department staff and personnel matters;
- Review of the collective bargaining agreement;
- Analysis of absenteeism and leave usage;
- Assessment of bus fleet and maintenance;
- Review of the age of the fleet, mileage, and required capital investment;
- Review of the district's practices regarding school bus replacement;
- Review of the adequacy of the fleet maintenance system;
- Review of part inventory control and reordering;
- Review of the preventive maintenance program;
- Review of vehicle inspection reports;
- Assessment of the extracurricular transportation services;
- Appropriateness of the budget and budget process for transporting students for extracurricular activities;
- Schedules and adherence to schedules.

A comprehensive and multidimensional analysis of opportunities for privatization as compared to the cost of self-operation will ultimately lead to a conclusion as to whether a district's transportation operation is viable. Given the political nature of school transportation services, it is also advantageous from this perspective for a district to contract with an outside firm specializing in identifying transportation efficiencies. The status quo is very powerful and managers may feel that they must defend their current system.

OUTSOURCING OF TRANSPORTATION

Current statistics indicate that approximately 30%–40% of school districts contract out for all or some of their school transportation services. Although privatization will not benefit all school districts, all districts should evaluate the option. The main reason to consider outsourcing is to improve service quality and to reduce costs. Public services should be held accountable for cost and be operationally competitive with the same services if provided by the private sector. Consideration of privatization at least demonstrates to the community a good faith attempt to assure equity and meet fiduciary responsibility to the public to utilize their financial resources as cost-effectively and efficiently as possible.

A review of transportation should include both an analysis of service quality as well as comparative costs, because a strict cost comparison with neighboring school districts' costs is generally not sufficient to ascertain the true comparative costs. As an example, if it is determined that the district is providing poor-quality service at a higher-than-reasonable cost, outsourcing should be seriously considered.

Although the district may give up a modicum of day-to-day control, it is outweighed by service improvement and reduced costs. If, on the other hand, the district is providing low-quality service at a low cost or a high level of service at a high cost, the decision to outsource is much less evident.

When considering outsourcing, the district should consider both the direct and the indirect costs associated with the provision of transportation services. In order to fully evaluate the feasibility of improving service quality and/or reducing transportation costs by outsourcing, the district should

- Determine its full cost of student transportation, including associated costs such as employee benefits (current and future), fuel, and insurances that may be budgeted in other departments;
- Prepare comprehensive bid specifications and aggressively market the bid;
- Identify current and future capital costs for vehicle replacement, maintenance equipment, and facilities;
- Evaluate the options for outsourcing, based on bid prices and comparable levels of service.

Although outsourcing may be a viable option, it must be carefully evaluated to guarantee that all of the district's transportation needs will be met. Even if outsourced, it is still the district's responsibility to provide safe and efficient transportation to all of its eligible students. Outsourcing can have the following benefits:

Advantages of Outsourcing Transportation Include:

- A renewed focus by district administrators on educational improvement;
- A reduction in capital planning for the replacement of school vehicles and corresponding reductions in insurance and other areas;
- A reduction in personnel and human resources issues, because the driving and supporting staff are now contractor employees;

- A future cost avoidance of ongoing health insurance and employee retirement costs;
- Elimination of indirect or hidden associated costs including payroll taxes, clerical and administrative support services, telephone, utilities, legal fees, and fuel tank testing and repairs;
- A reduction in district administrative support of transportation employees.

If a district deems it fiscally and programmatically advantageous to outsource, it should consider the following contractual provisos:

- A contract clause that is performance based as an incentive for increasing efficiency;
- A contract requirement to utilize computerized routing and scheduling;
- A contract requirement to maintain a cost accounting system to monitor efficiency and cost-effectiveness;
- A broad range of experience and expertise in providing school transportation services to different types of districts (problems can often be solved more quickly and effectively with prior experience);
- A contract performance clause requiring improved service quality with specific benchmarks;
- Development of a comprehensive contract with performance indicators and incentives for increased service quality and efficiency.

Disadvantages of Outsourcing Transportation Include:

- The district may have less control of the day-to-day operations and procedures;
- Public employees may lose their public employment and public employee benefits;
- Contractors will typically amortize their capital costs based upon the length of their contract and this cost can be high with short-term contracts;[2]
- If bid competition is not evident, the resulting cost of the contract may not meet the district's targeted savings;
- A contractor may underbid its competitors in order to acquire the contract in the hope of increasing the cost in subsequent years;
- If the bid specifications and contract language are vague, the contractor may try to take advantage of unclear or misleading information to raise the price subsequent to the award and/or during the contract;
- Additional services required during the contract may be higher than the anticipated price;
- Transportation services could be in jeopardy if the contractor experiences labor or collective bargaining disputes;

- The district could experience higher unemployment costs should its current drivers not join the contractor company.

TRANSPORTATION BIDDING

School districts want to minimize the number of vehicles necessary to safely and effectively transport students. However, contractors who are compensated on a cost per day per bus do not have an incentive to be cost-effective in minimizing the number of vehicles used because their profits are based on maximizing the number of vehicles. Somewhere between the multiple paradigms is a happy medium that will balance the needs of the school district and provide a fair and equitable investment for private contractors and their stakeholders.

Bidding Specifications

One effective strategy to optimize public bidding is to develop specifications that outline the needs of the district in such a way that will foster legitimate competition for a contract. Small- to medium-sized individual school districts are at definite disadvantage in this regard because they have a relatively small number of buses, and therefore do not necessarily generate interest from any of the large transportation companies. As previously stated, an effective strategy for bringing about significant efficiencies is coordinating bidding among several contiguous school districts and creating an economy of scale likely to garner interest from bus companies and contractors outside the immediate school district area.

Bidding Methodology

Among the bidding strategies that have proved to be effective is the offering of a multiyear contract, where the award is made based on the first year's cost only with subsequent cost-of-living adjustments (COLA) applied annually during the term of the contract. The annual increase is based upon the cost-of-living index determined annually by the US Bureau of Labor Statistics. Fuel costs should also be adjusted annually utilizing a fuel escalation/de-escalation, as determined by local tax-exempt fuel costs. The school district should award the bid to the lowest responsive and responsible bidder.

All the strategies require the district to share future economic conditions with the contractor, but also allow the contractor to base future bid costs on existing economic conditions. The school district then shares the economic risk with the contractor. The accommodations allow the contractor to focus on immediate current costs with the good faith agreement that they are protected from large-scale changes in economic conditions.

Based upon published trends, annual costs for both fuel and COLA can be determined early in the budgeting cycle. This methodology not only reduces the contract's initial cost but also provides for future cost avoidance, as the bidder/contractor need not build his or her own worst economic predictions into the initial cost structure.

CONCLUSION

Special education transportation is one of the most highly regulated and monitored transportation services. Because it is a related service under both IDEA and ADA, it is governed by the same laws and regulations that govern special education in general. As such, the type of transportation required for each student with disabilities is prescribed through the student's IEP process.

Therefore, special education transportation, like special education, is based on the needs of the individual student. Any individualized service is inherently more costly than group services, such as those transportation services provided to eligible general education students. Large buses with the capacity to transport seventy-five students are considerably less expensive to operate when they are operating with a relatively full load, on a per-student cost basis, than are small buses or vans transporting far fewer students.

School transportation services generally represent a significant amount of a school district's budget. Any cost reduction while providing high-quality services allows the district to invest greater financial resources in classroom-based education programs and services. Every public school district has fiduciary responsibility to be cost-effective in the utilization of financial resources provided by the community. The operation of a high-quality transportation system at an acceptable cost satisfies a sizable part of that responsibility.

Among the strategies districts can employ to mitigate the high cost of special education transportation are

- Multidistrict public bidding utilizing improved specifications;
- Utilization of computerized routing and scheduling programs;
- Multidistrict routing and scheduling and cost sharing among contiguous school districts for common placements;
- Regionalization of transportation services;
- Utilization of regular transportation whenever possible for students with disabilities;
- Requirement of only that level of special transportation necessary to the safe and efficient transportation of the student through the legal IEP process;
- Cost comparison with neighboring school districts;

- An independent efficiency study of transportation or technical services that may include the management of the public bidding process, including the development of improved bid specifications;
- Outsourced transportation services with terms that benefit both the district and the contractor-partner.

Multiple strategies may be employed to reduce or control the cost of special education transportation. In order to determine whether the current transportation system is both cost-effective and efficient, the district must determine whether the current system provides a satisfactory level of service at an acceptable cost. Oftentimes, this determination requires outside technical assistance from a source with expertise in both contracted as well as district self-operated transportation services.

Given the current economic climate, it is imperative that districts maximize their school transportation efficiencies. With finite financial resources, it is important to maximize the dollars going into the classroom and to minimize the dollars used for transportation, without compromising quality or safety.

REFERENCES

American Logistics Company (2010, June). *American Logistics Company Renews Transportation Services Contract with Washington County School District.* Press Release, Monday, June 28, 2010, 11:15, School Transportation News, Inter Net. http://www.stnonline.com/home/press-releases/2491-american-logistics-company-renews-transportation-services-contract-with-utahs-washington-county-school-district

Americans with Disabilities Act (ADA) of 1990, 42 U.S.C. §§ 12101–12213.

Ammon, T. (2010, January). "Transportation Consolidation: Pitfalls and Possibilities." *KEY Post*, 23, no. 2.

Individuals with Disabilities Education Act (IDEA), 20 U.S.C. Implementing Regulations at 34 C.F.R. § 300.2 (15) (a), § 300.24 (b) (15), § 104.43, § 104.37.

Individuals with Disabilities Education Act (IDEA), at 20 U.S.C. § 1401 (a) (22).

Labrie, R. (2010, November). "Report to the Rhode Island Legislature, Rhode Island Department of Elementary and Secondary Education, Rhode Island Statewide Transportation Project."

Lake, S. E. *An Overview of Special Education Transportation.* Palm Beach Gardens, FL: LRP Publications: 3–9, 15–17.

Management Partnership Services (2009, October). "Analysis of Student Transportation Operations, Middleton-Cross Plains Area School District, Outsourcing Analysis." 1–2, 4, 18.

Massachusetts Organization of Educational Collaborative (2009, August). "Special Education Task Force Report."

Rehabilitation Act of 1973, Section 504. United States Department of Education.

"School Bus Transportation, State Share of Transportation Budget" (2004–2005). New Jersey Department of Education, Camden County Office, Expenditures.

Texas School District Transportation Services (2010, December). "Establishing Efficient Bus Routes and Schedules." Texas Performance Review, Legislative Budget Board.

Texas School District Transportation Services (2010, December). "Evaluating Transportation Privatization." Texas Performance Review, Legislative Budget Board.

Texas School District Transportation Services (2010, December). "Operating Efficient Systems of School Transportation." Texas Performance Review, Legislative Budget Board.
"Transportation, Performance Audit." Panama City, FL, Panama City School District, (2011, May).

POINTS TO REMEMBER

- *School transportation services are one of the many services that school districts must provide as a bundle of special education and related services for students with disabilities.*
- *School transportation is one of the most highly regulated and monitored forms of transportation. Given the amount of law and regulation associated with the provision of special education services, including transportation as a related service, it is no small wonder why special education transportation is expensive.*
- *Whenever possible, students with disabilities should ride regular buses. Special buses should only be utilized when a student cannot access regular transportation services safely.*
- *When considering whether the transportation system is cost-effective and efficient, ask two questions: Is the service being provided satisfactory, and is the cost reasonable? An efficient transportation system is one that provides high-quality service at an acceptable cost.*
- *If the district's school transportation operation is providing a high level of service quality at a reasonable cost then there is no financial incentive to consider outsourcing or contracting out for school transportation services.*
- *Routing and scheduling probably has the single biggest impact on the efficiency of any transportation system. From the routes and schedules developed come both the number of vehicles required and the amount of driver time required to meet the district's and the students' transportation requirements.*
- *Public bidding for school transportation services should be utilized whenever possible. Legitimate competition can lead to lower costs and a higher quality of service.*

NOTES

1. State reimbursements for school transportation are generally done using a formula based on eligible rider criteria and a linear density model. Inefficient routes can result in a reduction of district reimbursement even though the costs may be increasing.

2. The district may/may not require new buses at the start of or during the contract. Fleet age and maximum mileage requirements should be specifically delineated in bid specifications and contracts.

References

American Logistics Company (2010, June). *American Logistics Company Renews Transportation Services Contract with Washington County School District.* Press Release, Monday, June 28, 2010, 11:15, School Transportation News, Inter Net. http://www.stnonline.com/home/press-releases/2491-american-logistics-company-renews-transportation-services-contract-with-utahs-washington-county-school-district

American Physical Therapy Association (2009). *Guidelines: Physical Therapy Scope of Practice.* www.apta.org.

American Speech-Language-Hearing Association (2007). *Scope of Practice in Speech Language Pathology.* www.asha.org.

Bowman, D. H. (2003). "Minnesota Scrambles to Revamp Standards." *Education Week*, 22, no. 23: 15, 20.

Brigham, F. J., W. E. Gustashaw III, A. L. Wiley, and M. Brigham (2004). "Research in the Wake of the No Student Left Behind Act: Why the Controversies Will Continue and Some Suggestions for Controversial Research." *Behavioral Disorders*, 29, no. 3.

Center for Special Education Finance (2004). (Originally published February 1998.) *What Are We Spending on Special Education in the United States.* no. 8.

Chamber, J. G. et al. (2004, May). *Special Education Expenditure Project.* Office of Special Education Programs, US Department of Education.

Clayton, J., M. Burdge, M., A. Denham, H. L. Kleinert, and J. Kearns, J. (2006). "A Four-Step Process for Accessing the General Curriculum for Students with Significant Cognitive Disabilities." *Teaching Exceptional Children*, 38, no. 5.

Courtade, G. R., and B. L. Ludlow (2007). "Ethical Issues and Severe Disabilities: Programming for Students and Preparation for Teachers." *Rural Special Education Quarterly*, 27, no. 1/2.

Daniel, P. T. (2008). "'Some Benefit' or 'Maximum Benefit': Does the No Child Left Behind Act Render Greater Educational Entitlement to Students with Disabilities." *Journal of Law and Education*, 37, no. 3: 347.

David, K. (2005). "IDEA 2004, P.L. 108-446: Impact on Physical Therapy Related Services." Fact Sheet Summary, www.apta.org.

Donlevy, J. (2002). "Teachers, Technology and Training: No Child Left Behind: In Search of Equity for All Children." *International Journal of Instructional Media*, 29, no. 3.

Earles-Vollrath, T. L. (2004). "IDEA 1997 and Related Services." *Intervention in School and Clinic*, 39, no. 4.

Englert, K., D. Fries, B. Goodwin, and M. Martin-Glenn (2003). *Understanding How Superintendents Use Data in a New Environment of Accountability.* Institute of Education Sciences, US Department of Education.

Essex, N. L. (2008). *School Law and the Public Schools: A Practical Guide for Educational Leaders*. 4th ed. Boston: Pearson Education.

Gartin, B. C., and N. L. Murdick (2005). "IDEA 2004: The IEP." *Remedial and Special Education*, 26, no. 6.

Gray, L. H. (2005). "No Child Left Behind: Opportunities and Threats." *The Journal of Negro Education*, 74, no. 2.

Hall, S. (2007). "NCLB and IDEA: Optimizing Success for Students with Disabilities." *Perspectives on Language and Literacy*, 33, no. 1.

Hess, F. M., and C. E. Finn, Jr. (2004). "Inflating the Life Rafts of NCLB: Making Public School Choice and Supplemental Services Work for Students in Troubled Schools." *Phi Delta Kappan*, 86, no. 1: 34.

Huefner, D. S. (2008). "Updating the FAPE Standard under IDEA." *Journal of Law and Education*, 37, no. 3.

Hyatt, K. J. (2007). "The New IDEA: Changes, Concerns, and Questions." *Intervention in School and Clinic*, 42, no. 3.

Imber, M., and T. Van Geel (2010). *Education Law*. 4th ed. New York: Routledge.

Jameson, J. M., and D. S. Heufner (2006). "'Highly Qualified' Special Educators and the Provision of a Free Appropriate Public Education to Students with Disabilities." *Journal of Law and Education*, 35, no. 1.

Keller-Allen, C. (2009, September). "Superintendent Leadership: Promoting General and Special Education Collaboration." *InForum*, US Department of Education.

Klotz, M. B., and L. Nealis (2005). "The New IDEA: A Summary of Significant Reforms." National Association of School Psychologists.

Mandlawitz, M. (2007). *What Every Teacher Should Know about IDEA 2004 Laws and Regulations*. Boston: Pearson Education.

McKenzie, A., and A. Bishop (2009, October). "Outsourcing Special Education Services." *The School Administrator*. Fairfax, VA: American Association of School Administrators.

Means, J. (2006). "The Impact of IDEA 04 and NCLB on Speech and Language Related Services: How Do We Meet the Challenges." *Forum on Public Policy: A Journal of the Oxford Round Table*.

Mele-McCarthy, J. A. (2007a). "Approaches to Assessment: IDEA and NCLB." *Perspectives on Language and Literacy*, 33, no. 1.

Mele-McCarthy, J. A. (2007b). "NCLB Assessment of Accountability: Good Teaching or Teaching to the Test?" *Perspectives on Language and Literacy*, 33, no. 1.

Moore-Brown, B. (2004). "Becoming Proficient in the Lessons of No Child Left Behind." *Perspectives on School-Based Issues*, 5, no. 1: 7–10.

National Education Association website, www.nea.org.

"Occupational Therapy in School Settings" (2010). www.aota.org.

Packer, J. (2007). "The NEA Supports Substantial Overhaul, Not Repeal, of NCLB." *Phi Delta Kappan*, 89, no. 4.

Rosenberg, M. S., P. T. Sindelar, and M. L. Hardman (2004). "Preparing Highly Qualified Teachers for Students with Emotional or Behavioral Disorders: The Impact of NCLB and IDEA." *Behavioral Disorders*, 29, no. 3.

Schuman, D. (2004). *American Schools, American Teachers: Issues and Perspectives*. Boston: Pearson Education.

Biographies

Our "community of practitioners" who contributed their time and effort to this initiative:

COEDITORS

Peter J. Bittel, EdD

Dr. Bittel is cofounder and chief executive officer of Futures Education, a company providing special education and clinical services and management to districts across the country. Dr. Bittel is a speech and language pathologist and has more than thirty-five years of executive leadership experience in the areas of special education, rehabilitation, and developmental disabilities. He has taught at the primary, secondary, college, and graduate levels. He serves as a trustee at American International College in Springfield, Massachusetts.

Nicholas D. Young, PhD, EdD

Dr. Young has worked in diverse roles in education for more than twenty years, serving as a director of student services, principal, graduate professor, higher education administrator, and superintendent of schools. He holds numerous degrees from Austin Peay State University, Westfield State University, Western New England University, Union Institute and University, and the American International College, including a PhD in educational administration and an EdD in psychology. Dr. Young previously served as the president of the Massachusetts Association of School Superintendents, completed a distinguished Fulbright Program focused on Japanese educational systems, and was recognized as the Massachusetts Superintendent of the Year in 2010.

He has served for more than twenty-seven years to date in the US Army and US Army Reserves, and he is currently the commanding officer for the 405th Combat Support Hospital, USAR, located in West Hartford, Connecticut. Dr. Young is a frequent presenter at state, national, and international conferences and has published widely on a number of topics in education, leadership, and psychology.

CHAPTER CONTRIBUTORS

Peter Davies, MA, Special Education Diploma

Mr. Davies is a qualified British school inspector (special education), and has worked in school and district accountability for more than ten years in the United States. He has established special education programs and reviewed alternative provision and numerous special schools in the United Kingdom and the United States. He is a graduate of Cambridge University and holds a diploma (special education) from the Oxford University Department of Educational Studies. He currently works from Storrs, Connecticut, and Nanyuki, Kenya.

Brian Edwards, MEd, ABD

As the chief operating officer and chief financial officer of Futures Education, Mr. Edwards has been integral in the reengineering of the delivery systems of school districts, resulting in better outcomes for students, promotion of best pedagogical and clinical practices, and greater fiscal resources for Futures' partners. More specifically, Mr. Edwards has been at the forefront in the redesign in the delivery of occupational and physical therapy services in the District of Columbia Public Schools that has entailed a reconstitution of practice patterns, intensive professional development, and ongoing support in the field.

Erin Edwards, MA, CCC/SLP, ABD

Ms. Edwards is cofounder and president of the Futures HealthCore. Prior to cofounding Futures, she served as vice president of rehabilitation for a thriving rehabilitation business. Prior to that, she served as the director of clinical services for a national health care company. Throughout her career, Ms. Edwards has held several executive leadership positions in the areas of early intervention and mental retardation/developmental disabilities in a variety of clinical settings including schools, skilled nursing facilities, home care, outpatient clinics, and other community-based programs. Ms. Edwards has been a practicing speech and language pathologist for nearly twenty-five years, and continues to practice in addition to her management responsibilities.

George David Jack, MEd, MBA

Mr. Jack holds a bachelor of science in financial management from Rensselaer Polytechnic Institute, a master's degree in educational administration from Rivier College, and an MBA from Southern New Hampshire University. He began his career as a social studies teacher in Methuen Public Schools followed by five years in a private high school, holding several positions in his tenure including biology teacher, athletic director, and assistant principal and financial officer. In 1985, Mr. Jack returned to the public school setting as a business administrator for the Salem Public Schools in Salem, New Hampshire. In 1986, he was appointed to a similar position, assistant superintendent for business, for the Derry Public Schools in Derry, New Hampshire, where he remained for sixteen years. In 2001, he returned to Massachusetts as the business administrator for the Lincoln Public Schools where he remained until 2005, when he accepted a position in Amesbury, Massachusetts, as an assistant superintendent for business and human resources.

Mr. Jack was appointed superintendent of schools in Amesbury in 2009 until he retired in 2011. Additionally Mr. Jack has taught graduate-level courses at Cambridge College and Salem State College.

Richard Labrie, MEd

Mr. Labrie has more than thirty-five years of educational administrative experience at both the secondary and post-secondary levels. His primary areas of expertise include educational needs assessments, program planning, development, program implementation, and evaluation. He has earned a master's degree in educational administration and a baccalaureate degree in educational administration, and completed graduate coursework in educational policy, research, and administration, as well as law. For seventeen years, Mr. Labrie held the position of executive director of the Lower Pioneer Valley Educational Collaborative, the largest and most multipurpose of the Massachusetts educational collaborative. Prior to that, he was executive director of the South Berkshire Educational Collaborative in Great Barrington, Massachusetts. He has also held research positions with Technical Education Research Centers in Newton and with Public Management Systems in Springfield and Cambridge, Massachusetts.

Mr. H. Larson, PhD

Dr. Larson holds a bachelor of science in mathematics education and a master of science in secondary education, both from the University of Bridgeport, Bridgeport, Connecticut, and a doctorate in curriculum and instruction from the University of Connecticut. He began his career in education as a mathematics teacher in the Trumbull, Connecticut, Public Schools. In 1972, he took a position as an assistant principal at Southington High School in Connecticut and in 1976 as principal of North Branford High School in Connecticut. He then held positions as assistant superintendent of schools in Southington, Connecticut, and superintendent of schools in Middletown, Connecticut. Before retiring in 2008, he became executive director of the Connecticut Association of Public School Superintendents.

Herbert Levine, PhD

Dr. Levine holds a bachelor of science in history and a master's degree in education administration from Boston State College, and a doctor of philosophy from Boston College. He began his career in education in the Revere Public Schools where he was a history and English teacher and then held the position of teacher/supervisor of the Alternative High School Program. He followed his positions in the Revere Public Schools with positions as assistant headmaster/dean of students at South Boston High School; principal of Timberline Regional High School in Plaistow, New Hampshire; and principal of Chelmsford High School in Chelmsford, Massachusetts. In 1995, he became deputy superintendent of schools in Wakefield, Massachusetts, and then in 1998, superintendent of schools in Salem, Massachusetts, from which position he retired in 2005. In 2004, he became executive director of the New England Association of School Superintendents, a position he continues to hold. He served as special assistant to the lieutenant governor and overall coordinator of Recovery High Schools from 2005–2007 and then as interim superintendent of schools in Blackstone, Massachusetts, from 2007–2008. Dr. Levine held a position as an adjunct associate professor at Boston State College and is currently a professor at Salem State College and Endicott College.

Christine N. Michael, PhD

Dr. Michael is a more than thirty-year educational veteran with a variety of professional experiences. She holds degrees from Brown University, Rhode Island College, Union Institute and University, and the University of Connecticut, where she earned a PhD in education and human development and family relations. Previous work has included middle and high school teaching, higher education administration, college teaching, educational consulting, literacy development, Head Start, Upward Bound, GED preparation, and the federal Trio programs. She is a licensed principal and superintendent in the State of New York. Her interest in small and rural schools is currently expressed through work in rural Kentucky, the Western Slope of Colorado, Standing Rock Indian Reservation schools, and the Adirondack Mountains of New York.

Michael Neiman, PhD, CCC/SLP

In his capacity as vice president of clinical programs, Dr. Neiman is responsible for the management of therapists, contract sites, and program development. He has been a practicing speech and language pathologist for nearly fifteen years. In that time, he has provided speech therapy services in a variety of settings including hospitals, nursing homes, schools, and day rehabilitation programs. In addition to his clinical experience, Dr. Neiman has been a manager of numerous rehabilitation facilities and is currently an adjunct professor at Elms College in Chicopee, Massachusetts. He continues to provide clinical services, in addition to his management responsibilities. Dr. Neiman holds a doctorate in adult neurogenic communication disorders.

Wendy C. Reed, Esq

Ms. Reed was admitted to the Pennsylvania Bar in 1983. She earned a doctor of law from Georgetown Law Center and a bachelor of arts from the University of Pennsylvania. She also attended Cambridge University as a graduate student on a Thouron Scholarship. Currently, Ms. Reed practices in her own firm, the Law Offices of Wendy C. Reed, specializing in special education law and also consulting in that field.

Dominick C. Vita, PhD

Dr. Vita holds a bachelor of arts in history with a minor in psychology and education from Assumption College, a master of arts from Fairfield University, and a doctorate from Heed University. Dr. Vita began his career in education as a teacher at Cathedral High School in Bridgeport, Connecticut. A few years later he joined the Norwalk, Connecticut, Public Schools as a school counselor. He then held positions as assistant supervisor of special education and principal administrator; acting director of adult education; supervisor of special education; director of student services and special education in the Norwalk, Connecticut, Public Schools; director of pupil services in Fall Village, Connecticut; superintendent of schools in Bethany, Connecticut; and, finally, superintendent of schools in Litchfield, Connecticut, where he remained until October 2008 before retiring.